Crime and Anti-Social Behaviour

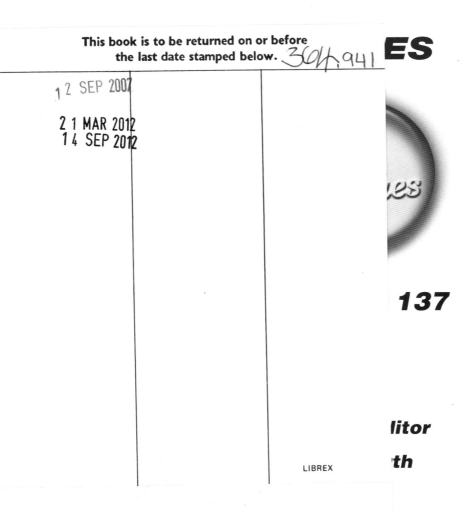

ES

137

litor

'th

Independence

Educational Publishers
Cambridge

First published by Independence
PO Box 295
Cambridge CB1 3XP
England

British Library Cataloguing in Publication Data
Crime and Anti-Social Behaviour – (Issues Series)
I. Firth, Lisa II. Series
364.9'41

ISBN 978 1 86168 389 2

Printed in Great Britain
MWL Print Group Ltd

Cover
The illustration on the front cover is by
Simon Kneebone.

CONTENTS

WOODMILL HIGH SCHOOL

Introduction

Crime and Anti-Social Behaviour is the one hundred and thirty-seventh volume in the **Issues** series. The aim of this series is to offer up-to-date information about important issues in our world.

Crime and Anti-Social Behaviour looks at crime issues, young people and crime, and crime solutions.

The information comes from a wide variety of sources and includes:
Government reports and statistics
Newspaper reports and features
Magazine articles and surveys
Website material
Literature from lobby groups
and charitable organisations.

It is hoped that, as you read about the many aspects of the issues explored in this book, you will critically evaluate the information presented. It is important that you decide whether you are being presented with facts or opinions. Does the writer give a biased or an unbiased report? If an opinion is being expressed, do you agree with the writer?

Crime and Anti-Social Behaviour offers a useful starting-point for those who need convenient access to information about the many issues involved. However, it is only a starting-point. Following each article is a URL to the relevant organisation's website, which you may wish to visit for further information.

* * * * *

Crime and justice

Information from the Centre for Crime and Justice Studies

Crime, its causes, and how it is dealt with, are some of the biggest issues in Britain today. Politicians and political parties can win or lose power depending on how well we think they are doing on the issue of crime. Not a day passes without some criminal justice story featuring in the news. This article is intended to give you some foundation in this important area.

A 'criminal offence' includes any infringement of the criminal law, from murder to riding a bicycle without lights

What is crime?

As a starting point, crime may be defined as an act or omission prohibited or punished by law. A 'criminal offence' includes any infringement of the criminal law, from murder to riding a bicycle without lights. This is quite separate from the 'civil law'. In the civil law, proceedings are begun by persons, companies, or organisations claiming to have suffered a breach. Prosecutions in the criminal law are begun by an agency of the State.

⇨ In England, criminal cases are cited as The Crown versus Mr X (and are written as R. v. Mr X, the R. standing for Regina, the Queen).

What is classified as a crime is supposed to reflect the values of society and to reinforce those values. If an act is regarded as harmful to society or its citizens, it is often, but not always (take smoking and drinking for example), classified as a criminal offence.

The United Kingdom relies on Parliament to classify what acts are criminal and what the penalties for these criminal offences are; the idea being that those most harmful to us carry the harshest penalties. In other words, crime is what the government says it is. Of course, what this means is that what is a crime one year might not be a crime the next, and that penalties for crime can also change a great deal.

For example:

⇨ In 1966 sex between two twenty-one-year-old men was illegal. In 1967, after the passing of the Sexual Offences Act, it was legal.

⇨ In 2002 you could be sent to jail for simple possession of marijuana, now you cannot.

⇨ In 1919 you were free to possess and consume opium (of which heroin is a derivative), but in 1920 it became illegal without a doctor's prescription.

Politics, politicians, and crime

What a person's or a political party's position on issues relating to crime is may influence greatly their prospects of getting elected. This does not mean, however, that the people in power or the political parties are that far from each other in their stances.

⇨ Over the last ten years the crime rate has fallen.

⇨ In that same period the United Kingdom's prison population has rapidly grown.

⇨ This is despite the fact that prison is the most costly response to crime (at about £300 a night) and rates of reoffending of released prisoners are extremely high.

⇨ We now imprison at a greater rate than any other country in the European Union, we imprison more children than anyone else, and the female prison population has doubled in the last ten years.

⇨ In the last ten years we have been governed by both the Labour Party and the Conservative Party.

So what is going on?

Surveys have shown that Britons are becoming increasingly afraid of being a victim of crime when the actual chance of being a victim of crime is at its lowest in 20 years. In response politicians promise to be tough on crime and, in some cases, on the causes of crime too. Here are the main policies of the three main parties:

- Labour: Has overseen the greatest portion of the growth of the prison population. Boasts record numbers of police supported by new 'community support officers' and 'tough new laws'. Has recently focused on crime committed by young people, anti-social behaviour, and 'persistent and prolific offenders'.
- Conservative: Promise a 'war on crime' and the building of more prisons. Believes that prison sentences should be longer and intends to do away with early release schemes for prisoners. Claims that police performance is slipping and police are hampered by form-filling and red tape. Wants to recruit 5,000 more police officers per year.
- Liberal Democrat: Would like new 'tough liberalism' to be introduced into criminal justice policy. This includes more training and education for prisoners, selling inner-city prisons and building 'modern prisons' outside of city centres, and introducing 'community justice panels' staffed by members of communities to determine sentences for some offenders.

Crime and the media

Two-thirds of the country believe that crime is rising when it is doing the opposite. So why are we getting it so wrong?

Most of us get our information about crime from the popular media: television and radio news, and the newspapers. Three-quarters of people get information about the criminal justice system from television or radio news, and about one-half said that they get information from television documentaries, local and tabloid newspapers.

BUT: only 6 per cent of people think that their main source of news about the criminal justice system is inaccurate.

THIS MEANS: the vast majority of us trust our news sources, SO what these sources say is very important.

The fact is that sensational stories attract the most people. The most sensational stories involve the most

shocking crimes (murder, rape, and any crime against children), or the most prolific or exceptional offenders. But these are only a small minority of crimes. And the amount of time and space covering crime issues continues to rise. As does our fear of crime.

Image courtesy of Carl Silver

The Home Office estimates that the total cost of crime in Britain each year is £59.9 billion

The cost of crime

The Home Office estimates that the total cost of crime in Britain each year is £59.9 billion. This figure represents much more than just the value of goods that may have been stolen, it includes:
- Spending on security to prevent crime;
- The cost of treating victims of crime in hospital;
- Lost wages; and
- The cost of running the criminal justice system – courts, police, prisons, and all.

With all that money being lost and spent, there is also plenty of it to be made. More and more the government is looking to private companies to provide services within the criminal justice system:
- There are now ten private prisons in the United Kingdom.
- These prisons hold 9 per cent of the prison population.
- They are run by multinational companies such as Group 4, Premier, Serco, Sodexho and Securicor.
- In September 2003 Serco estimated that its existing UK prisons and correctional services contracts were valued at £2 billion.
- All the Immigration Detention Centres are privately operated.

- These and other companies also design and build prisons, transport prisoners, run holding cells in courts, supply food, supply the police with equipment and so on. Crime is big business.

The criminal justice system and business are linked in other ways too. For example, the Prison Service is seeking to increase partnerships with industries, supplying machinery and a workforce in return for training.

Did you know . . . ?
- Emile Durkheim, one of the founders of modern sociology, believed that crime was important to the well-being of society because challenges to established moral and legal laws (deviance and crime, respectively) acted to unify the law-abiding and reinforce their values.
- The Inside-Out Trust runs a programme in Her Majesty's Prison Wandsworth in which prisoners can work on repairing bicycles that are then sent to Africa for use there.

Useful links
- http://www.inside-out.org.uk – The Inside-Out trust develops prison projects based on restorative justice principles. Prisoners learn new skills which they willingly use to provide goods and services to disadvantaged people all over the world; new skills which should improve their own employment prospects after release.
- http://www.homeoffice.gov.uk/crime/index.html – The Home Office's crime website.

See what the three main parties have to say:
- http://www.labour.org.uk/crime04/ – The Labour Party
- http://www.libdems.org.uk/index.cfm/page.folders/section.policy/folder.policy_papers – The Liberal Democrats
- http://www.conservatives.com/policies – The Conservative Party

- The above information is reprinted with kind permission from the Centre for Crime and Justice Studies. Visit www.crimeinfo.org.uk for more information.

© CCJS

Crime in the UK

Information from the Economic and Social Research Council

Crime

Crime can be defined as an offence against an individual or the state, which is punishable by law. A person who commits an offence that breaks the law is a criminal.

The crime picture in the UK

In the UK there are two key sources of data that provide information about crime. These are the British Crime Survey (BCS) and police-recorded crime figures. According to the Home Office these are a complementary series that together provide a better picture of crime than could be obtained from either series alone.

Police-recorded crime figures provide a measure of well-reported crimes, and are an important indicator of police workload. They can also be used for local crime pattern analysis; however they often under-estimate petty offences which go unreported and sexual and domestic crimes.

For the offences it covers and the victims within its scope, the BCS gives a more complete estimate of crime in England and Wales, since it covers both unreported and unrecorded crime. It also gives a more reliable indication of trends in crime as BCS estimates are unaffected by changes in levels of reporting to the police, or in police recording. However it does not cover offences perpetrated by or against corporate bodies.

Crime levels in the UK

According to British Crime Survey (BCS) Interviews survey in 2005/6, it is estimated that there were approximately 10.9 million crimes against adults living in private households in England and Wales.

This represents an increase of one per cent compared with the estimate based on interviews in 2004/5, equivalent to about 60,000 crimes. This change is not statistically significant. There were 5.6 million crimes recorded by the English and Welsh police in 2005/6, a decrease of one per cent compared with 2004/5. Since the peak in 1995, BCS crime in England and Wales has fallen by 44 per cent, with vehicle crime and burglary falling by more than half and violent crime falling by over a third during this period.

In Scotland during 2005/6 there were 0.4 million recorded crimes, a decrease of five per cent on 2004/5. In Scotland, the latest non-police crime figures available are from the 2003 Scottish Crime and Victimisation Survey. This estimated that 0.9 million crimes were committed against households and individuals between April 2003 and March 2004. In Northern Ireland there were about 125,000 offences in 2005/6, an increase of four per cent on 2004/5.

Detection rates in the UK

Detection rates, in their broadest terms, refer to crimes 'cleared up' by the police. Detection rates refer to crimes, rather than offenders. For example, if six offenders are involved in a robbery this counts as one crime.

In 2005/6 there were around 1.5 million detected crimes in England and Wales. Some other crimes may have had a suspect identified, but did not meet the definition of detected crime. The detection rate in 2005/6 in England and Wales was 27 per cent, up slightly from 2004/5. This means that just over one in four crimes were 'cleared up'. Drug offences had the highest detection rate at 93 per cent for 2005/6; criminal damage and burglary were the least likely to be detected.

In Scotland, 46 per cent of recorded crimes were 'cleared up'. In Northern Ireland, the clearance rate was 31 per cent.

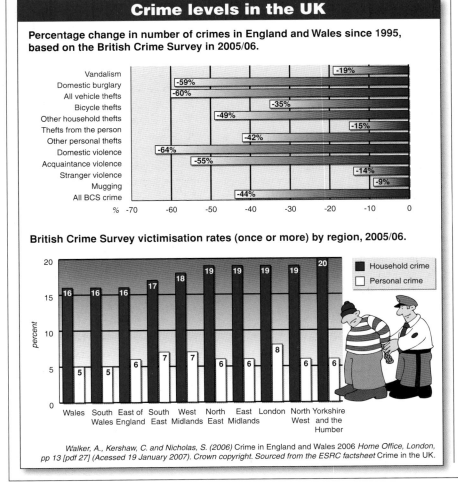

Crime levels in the UK

Percentage change in number of crimes in England and Wales since 1995, based on the British Crime Survey in 2005/06.

- Vandalism: -19%
- Domestic burglary: -59%
- All vehicle thefts: -60%
- Bicycle thefts: -35%
- Other household thefts: -49%
- Thefts from the person: -15%
- Other personal thefts: -42%
- Domestic violence: -64%
- Acquaintance violence: -55%
- Stranger violence: -14%
- Mugging: -9%
- All BCS crime: -44%

British Crime Survey victimisation rates (once or more) by region, 2005/06.

Legend: Household crime / Personal crime

Region	Household crime	Personal crime
Wales	16	5
South Wales	16	5
East of England	16	6
South East	17	7
West Midlands	18	7
North East	19	6
East Midlands	19	6
London	19	8
North West	19	6
Yorkshire and the Humber	20	6

Walker, A., Kershaw, C. and Nicholas, S. (2006) Crime in England and Wales 2006 Home Office, London, pp 13 [pdf 27] (Acessed 19 January 2007). Crown copyright. Sourced from the ESRC factsheet Crime in the UK.

Police force detection rates varied between 20 per cent (British Transport Police) and 45 per cent (Dyfed-Powys), although several factors influence a force's ability to detect crimes, most notable the area's crime mix. This is the idea that all crimes are not equal. Different areas have varying levels of each crime and each crime has varying detection rates.

Victims of crimes

Household crime victimisation rates varied from 20 per cent of households in the Yorkshire and the Humber region to 16 per cent in Wales, South West England and Eastern England. Personal crime varied less: in the London region, 8 per cent of people had been a victim of personal crime compared with 5 per cent of people in Wales and the South West of England.

Between April 1999 and December 2005 9,853 ASBOs were issued in England and Wales

---

Estimating international comparisons of crime rates is very difficult, given different legal systems, different policing arrangements and different statistical collection and recording procedures. The World Health Organisation attempted to compare homicide (Murder) rates internationally. The homicide rate per 100,000 population in England and Wales (0.6) is the lowest recorded by WHO (equal to that of Japan). However, homicide rates in medieval England were far higher, with estimates for the thirteenth and fourteenth centuries of 23 homicides per 100,000 population.

Young people aged 16-24 were most at risk of being a victim of violent crime in England and Wales in 2005/6. Men in this age group were more likely to be a victim than women. Domestic violence was the only category where the risk of violent crime was higher for women. Older people had a much lower risk of becoming a victim of violent crime, particularly the over 65s.

Households most at risk of burglary in England and Wales were those without any security measures. In addition, households where the head was unemployed, a single parent, aged 16-24 and with low income were at higher-than-average risk.

Anti-social behaviour

Anti-Social Behaviour Orders (ASBOs) have been introduced recently across the United Kingdom in an attempt to control behaviour which is perceived as causing alarm, distress or harassment to others but which might not necessarily be prosecuted as a criminal offence. It is granted by the courts following an application by the police or local authority.

Between April 1999 and December 2005 9,853 ASBOs were issued in England and Wales. ASBOs were introduced into Scotland in October 2004.

⇨ The above information is reprinted with kind permission from the Economic and Social Research Council. Visit www.esrc.ac.uk for more information.

© Economic and Social Research Council

Crime in England and Wales

Quarterly update to September 2006 – main points

⇨ The risk of being a victim of crime as measured by the British Crime Survey (BCS), at 24 per cent, has increased by one percentage point compared with the year to September 2005 (23%). This is still considerably lower than the peak of 40 per cent recorded by the survey in 1995.

⇨ The number of crimes recorded by the police fell by three per cent for the period July to September 2006 compared with the same quarter a year earlier.

⇨ There was no statistically significant change in BCS violent crime for interviews in year ending September 2006 compared with the previous year. Recorded violent crime for July to September 2006 showed a one per cent decrease over the same period in 2005.

⇨ BCS vehicle thefts and domestic burglary remained stable compared with interviews in the year to September 2005. In the latest quarter, recorded domestic burglary fell by three per cent, and recorded vehicle crime by four per cent.

⇨ BCS interviews in the 12 months to September 2006 showed an 11 per cent increase in the number of incidents of vandalism, while recorded crime showed a one per cent rise in criminal damage.

⇨ In the year to September 2006, there were a provisional 9,728 firearm offences, 14 per cent fewer than the previous year.

⇨ BCS interviews showed that there was no change in the overall measure of levels of perceived anti-social behaviour, however, individual strands showed some change. Levels of worry about burglary, car crime and violent crime have remained unchanged.

⇨ Levels of confidence in aspects of the criminal justice system have remained stable compared with the previous year. Confidence in the local police has improved

This update presents the most recent crime statistics from two different sources: the British Crime Survey (BCS) and police recorded crime. Both data sets represent the most up-to-date information, but they cover different time periods. The BCS results are from interviews conducted in the period October 2005 to September 2006; police recorded crime refers to the July to September 2006 quarter.

25 January 2007

⇨ The above information is reprinted with kind permission from the Home Office. Visit www.homeoffice.gov.uk for more information.

© Crown copyright

Britons most worried by crime

And government is least trusted to deal with it

People in Britain are more worried about crime and violence than other major countries in Europe and the US, according to an international survey by the Ipsos MORI International Social Trends Unit. The quarterly study – the International Social Trends Monitor – shows that over two in five British people find crime and violence one of the most worrying issues (43%), double the level in Germany (21%). Even Americans are far less concerned (27%).

Over two in five British people find crime and violence one of the most worrying issues (43%), double the level in Germany (21%). Even Americans are far less concerned (27%)

But the most worrying finding for the government is that, compared with other countries measured, British people have the lowest confidence in their government when it comes to crime. While less than a third of people in Britain believe Labour is capable of cracking down on crime (29%), confidence runs much higher in countries like Germany and Italy, where around half of people feel their government is capable (57% and 48% respectively).

Since Labour came into power, confidence in the government's policy on crime has mostly been in decline. In mid-1997, over two-thirds of people believed the government could reduce crime (68%), but by 2002, the proportion had more than halved (30%). Since then, Labour

has not improved their ratings, despite a significant focus on crime and policing.

Bobby Duffy, of the Ipsos MORI International Social Trends Unit, said: 'This major new study shows just how much of a challenge the British government faces in convincing people they can deal with crime and violence. Concern has been highest and confidence in the government lowest in Britain for many months, and there is no sign of this changing. And this is vitally important to overall government ratings – the trends show that competence in dealing with crime is one of the main things the government is judged on.'

Technical details

This quarterly study is carried out simultaneously in the US and the five biggest countries in the European Union: Germany, Spain, France, Italy and Great

Britain. Interviews are conducted by telephone using CATI (Computer Assisted Telephone Interviewing) among a representative sample of adults aged 18 years or more in each country. Data are weighted to reflect the known profile of each country's population.

In September 2006, Ipsos MORI interviewed a total of 5,970 people across the sample countries. The fieldwork dates and interview numbers were as follows: France (1,006): 25-27 September; Germany (1,000): 22-30 September; Italy (962): 22-29 September; Spain (1,000): 22-28 September; USA (1,000): 22-26 September; Great Britain (1,002): 22 September – 1 October. 6 November 2006

⇨ The above information is reprinted with kind permission from Ipsos MORI. Visit www.ipsos-mori.com for more information.

© Ipsos MORI

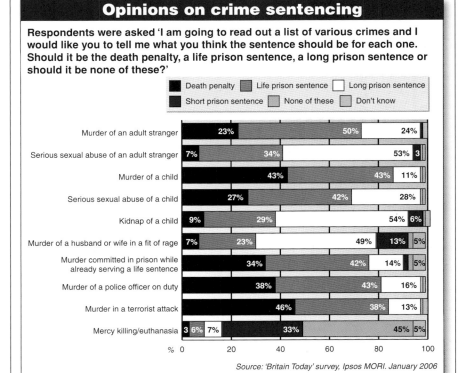

Opinions on crime sentencing

Respondents were asked 'I am going to read out a list of various crimes and I would like you to tell me what you think the sentence should be for each one. Should it be the death penalty, a life prison sentence, a long prison sentence or should it be none of these?'

- Death penalty
- Life prison sentence
- Long prison sentence
- Short prison sentence
- None of these
- Don't know

Murder of an adult stranger	23%	50%	24%
Serious sexual abuse of an adult stranger	7%	34%	53% 3
Murder of a child	43%	43%	11%
Serious sexual abuse of a child	27%	42%	28%
Kidnap of a child	9%	29%	54% 6%
Murder of a husband or wife in a fit of rage	7%	23%	49% 13% 5%
Murder committed in prison while already serving a life sentence	34%	42%	14% 5%
Murder of a police officer on duty	38%	43%	16%
Murder in a terrorist attack	46%	38%	13%
Mercy killing/euthanasia	3 6% 7%	33%	45% 5%

% 0   20   40   60   80   100

Source: 'Britain Today' survey, Ipsos MORI. January 2006

Britain tops European crime league

By Philip Johnston, Home Affairs Editor

Britain has one of the worst crime rates in Europe, a report said yesterday.

It is the most burgled country in Europe, has the highest level of assaults and above average rates of car theft, robbery and pickpocketing. Only Ireland has a worse record.

Estonia, Holland and Denmark make up the rest of the EU's five 'high-crime' nations. All had rates more than 30 per cent higher than the average. Spain, Hungary, Portugal and Finland had the lowest rates.

The report follows one of the most comprehensive law and order surveys in the EU. More than 40,000 people aged over 16 were questioned in 18 countries about their recent experiences of crime.

Factors associated with high levels of crime included urbanisation, a large number of young people in the population and a binge-drinking culture.

Risks of being assaulted were highest in the UK, Ireland, the Netherlands, Belgium, Sweden and Denmark and lowest in Italy, Portugal, Hungary, Spain and France.

Experiences with sexual violence were reported most often by women in Ireland, Sweden, Germany and Austria and least often in Hungary, Spain, France and Portugal.

One area where Britain came out well was on 'ethical' crime. People were asked whether they had been required to pay bribes to public officials over the past twelve months. Positive answers were given most often in Greece, Poland, Hungary and Estonia and bribe-seeking was least common in Finland, the UK, Sweden, the Netherlands and Ireland.

Rates of 'hate crimes' against minorities were most pronounced in France, Denmark, the UK and the Benelux countries, with the lowest levels in Italy, Portugal, Greece and Austria.

The European Crime and Safety Survey, published in Brussels yesterday, was a joint venture between the United Nations, the European Commission and the Gallup polling organisation.

It suggests that the British public are somewhat inured to high crime and not 'over-concerned' about burglary and safety on the streets. We also tend to be happier with the police than people in many other countries.

Nearly one-third of EU citizens said they were afraid of burglary and did not feel safe on the streets

The British are also much more in favour of prison as a punishment. More than twice as many people think a serial burglar should go to prison than in other countries.

Overall, nearly one-third of EU citizens said they were afraid of burglary and did not feel safe on the streets.

The survey found that 'common crimes' like burglary and car theft had fallen across the EU, including Britain, but this was linked to higher levels of security reflected in increased sales of alarms and special door locks.

The Government said the survey was three years out of date. Tony McNulty, the Home Office Minister, said: 'We have concerns about its quality and the comparisons. It does not take account of any recent crime reduction measures to tackle alcohol misuse, the acquisitive crime campaign and tough new measures in the Violent Crime Reduction Act to tackle gun and knife crime.'

Robert Manchin, the chairman of Gallup Europe, said it involved 'perceptions' of safety and security based on people's actual experience of crime. It did not correlate to recorded crime statistics which were collected differently around the EU.

Nick Clegg, the Liberal Democrat spokesman, said the study exposed Britain as the 'sick man of Europe'.

David Davis, the shadow home secretary, said: 'This shows that, by any measure, we are doing badly. Ten years of failure have left the public more at risk from property crime and violent crime than any other comparable country in Europe.'

7 February 2007

Violence in the UK

Information from the Economic and Social Research Council

This information provides a statistical overview of violence in the UK. It is designed to introduce the topic rather than be a comprehensive summary. Other ESRC fact sheets that are related are *Crime in the UK*, *Human rights*, *Security and Terrorism in the UK*.

The World Health Organisation defines violence as:

'The intentional use of physical force or power, threatened or actual, against oneself, another person or against a group or community, that either results in or has a likelihood of resulting in injury, death, psychological harm, mal-development or deprivation.'

This article will provide a snapshot image of violence in society today, both locally and globally, with information on violent crime motivated by a person's ethnicity, sexual orientation and gender.

Violent crime

Between 2005 and 2006 there were approximately 2,349,000 violent incidents in England and Wales, according to the British Crime Survey (BCS). In the same period, the number of violent crimes reported to the police stood at 1,056,000, indicating that approximately only 45 per cent of violent crime gets reported. In Scotland, there were 15, 809 violent crimes in 2004/5.

By 2005/06 levels of violent crime had decreased by over 43 per cent from a recent high level in 1995.

Perceptions and risks of violence

The British Crime Survey found that in 2005, for each age group, women were over twice as likely to be worried about violent crime as men and this was especially apparent in the younger age groups; among 16- to 24-year-olds 32 per cent of women had high levels of worry compared with 12 per cent of men. Younger people were more likely than older people to have high levels of worry about violence. For example, 12 per

cent of men aged 16 to 24 years had high levels of worry about violent crime compared with seven per cent of those aged 65 to 74 years.

The overall risk of being a victim of violent crime in 2005/6 was 3.4 per cent

---

The BCS also found that the overall risk of being a victim of violent crime in 2005/6 was 3.4 per cent. Young men, aged 16 to 24, were most at risk, with 12.6 per cent experiencing a violent crime of some sort in the year prior to the survey. The risk of becoming a victim

of violent crime was considerably lower for older people for all types of violence. Domestic violence was the only category of violence for which the risks for women (0.6%) were higher than for men (0.2%). Risks of stranger and acquaintance violence were substantially greater for men than for women; 2.1 per cent of men were victims of stranger violence in 2005/6 interviews, compared with 0.7 per cent of women.

Killings and weapons

There were 765 homicides in 2005/6, a decrease of 12 per cent from the previous year.

This figure includes the 52 homicide victims of the 7 July London bombings. Homicide accounts for 0.06 per cent of recorded violent crime. A sharp instrument was the most common weapon used in killings followed by firearms. There were 46 homicides involving firearms in 2005/6, 40 per cent (or 31 offences) fewer than 2004/5.

Weapons were used in 22 per cent of all violent crimes reported in the BCS in 2005/6. The most common types of weapons used were knives (seven per cent of all incidents), hitting implements (seven per cent), and glass or bottles (four per cent).

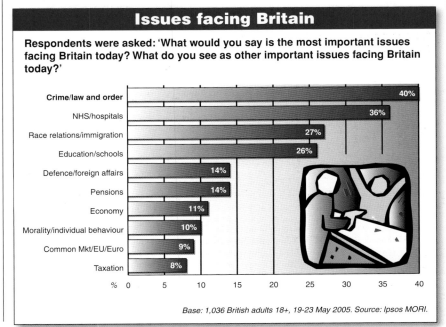

Issues facing Britain

Respondents were asked: 'What would you say is the most important issues facing Britain today? What do you see as other important issues facing Britain today?'

Issue	%
Crime/law and order	40%
NHS/hospitals	36%
Race relations/immigration	27%
Education/schools	26%
Defence/foreign affairs	14%
Pensions	14%
Economy	11%
Morality/individual behaviour	10%
Common Mkt/EU/Euro	9%
Taxation	8%

Base: 1,036 British adults 18+, 19-23 May 2005. Source: Ipsos MORI.

Violence to women

In 2005/6 there were 357,000 incidences of domestic violence in Britain, down from 989,000 in 1995. On average over 150 people (120 women, 30 men) are killed each year by a current or former partner. Statistically, one in four women and one in six men will experience domestic violence during their lifetime. For all incidences of domestic abuse reported to the police in 2004, only 21 per cent resulted in charges with 11 per cent leading to a conviction.

Police recorded 62,081 sexual offences in 2005/6

Sexual violence

Police recorded 62,081 sexual offences in 2005/6; of these 14,449 were rapes. 92 per cent of these were against women.

On average, the Rape Crisis Federation receives 50,000 calls a year. 90 per cent of callers identified the perpetrator as male who in 75 per cent of cases was known to the victim.

(Note that due to the introduction of the Sexual Offences Act 2003 in May 2004 there are substantial changes to the sexual offences. This means that figures for 2004/5 onwards are not comparable with those for previous years.)

Adults most at risk of violence

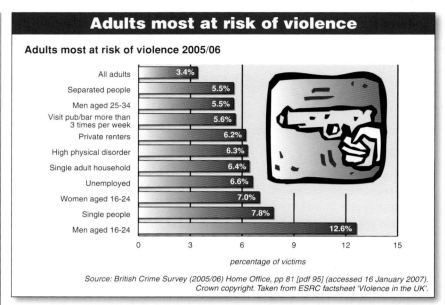

Adults most at risk of violence 2005/06

Category	Percentage
All adults	3.4%
Separated people	5.5%
Men aged 25-34	5.5%
Visit pub/bar more than 3 times per week	5.6%
Private renters	6.2%
High physical disorder	6.3%
Single adult household	6.4%
Unemployed	6.6%
Women aged 16-24	7.0%
Single people	7.8%
Men aged 16-24	12.6%

percentage of victims

Source: British Crime Survey (2005/06) Home Office, pp 81 [pdf 95] (accessed 16 January 2007). Crown copyright. Taken from ESRC factsheet 'Violence in the UK'.

Alcohol and violence

According to the BCS, there were 1,029,000 violent incidents where the victim believed the offender or offenders to be under the influence of alcohol in 2005/6. 46 per cent of incidents of domestic violence were committed by a perpetrator under the influence of alcohol. The severity of violence inflicted on the victim is linked to the quantity of alcohol consumed. Among 142 imprisoned rapists in the UK, 37 per cent were 'alcohol dependent' at the time of interview.

Suicide (self-directed violence)

In the UK as a whole in 2004, there were 5,906 suicides in adults aged 15 and over, which represented one per cent of the total of all UK deaths. Almost three-quarters of these suicides were among men. Suicide rates differ dramatically between countries globally, but in all cases men were much more likely to commit suicide than women.

Homophobic violence

The Metropolitan Police alone reported 11,799 incidents of racist and religious hate crime and 1,359 incidents of homophobic hate crime in the 12 months to January 2006.

However, the police estimate that most racist and religious hate crime, and as much as 90 per cent of homophobic crime, goes unreported because victims are too frightened or embarrassed to let someone know.

Racist violence

In 2002/3, adults from a Mixed Race or Asian background were more likely than those from other ethnic groups to be victims of crime in England and Wales. Almost half (46 per cent) of adults of Mixed Race had been the victim of a crime in the previous 12 months. This compared with 30 per cent of Asians. Black adults and those from the 'Chinese or other' group experienced similar levels of crime to White people. Racially-motivated incidents represented 12 per cent of all crime against minority ethnic people compared with 2 per cent for white people.

⇨ Information from the Economic and Social Research Council. Visit www.esrc.ac.uk for more information.
© ESRC

Suicide (self-directed violence)

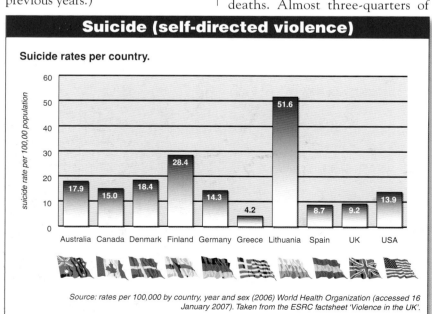

Suicide rates per country.

Country	Rate per 100,000
Australia	17.9
Canada	15.0
Denmark	18.4
Finland	28.4
Germany	14.3
Greece	4.2
Lithuania	51.6
Spain	8.7
UK	9.2
USA	13.9

suicide rate per 100,00 population

Source: rates per 100,000 by country, year and sex (2006) World Health Organization (accessed 16 January 2007). Taken from the ESRC factsheet 'Violence in the UK'.

Victims of crime reject notion of retribution

⇨ *Survey shows support for non-custodial sentences*
⇨ *Majority back face-to-face meetings with offenders*

By Alan Travis,
Home Affairs Editor

The notion that victims of crime are strong supporters of jail as the best approach to deterring petty criminals is challenged today with a poll showing that almost two-thirds believe that prison does not stop them reoffending.

The unique ICM poll of crime victims shows that a clear majority believe that making offenders carry out unpaid work in the community is a better alternative to a short prison sentence.

The survey, commissioned by Victim Support and the thinktank Smart Justice, shows that the overwhelming majority of crime victims believe that the best ways to curb non-violent crime are to provide more activities for young people, ensure they are better supervised by their parents, and provide more treatment for drug and mental health problems.

The ICM poll asked crime victims about the best ways of curbing non-violent crimes such as shoplifting, car theft and vandalism. It found that more than half of victims (53%) did not feel the criminal justice system takes account of their needs.

Peter Dunn, Victim Support's head of research, said: 'Victims are often assumed to be vengeful towards offenders and favour harsh punishments.

'This is misleading. Most victims, while feeling angry about what has happened to them, want the offender to stop offending both against them and against other people.'

He said the research showed that many victims were interested in constructive work being done with offenders to tackle the causes of crime.

Lucie Russell, of Smart Justice, said the poll was the first of crime victims, and it was clear they did not believe that prison produced law-abiding citizens: 'The survey proves that victims don't want retribution; they want a system that protects the next victim.'

The survey showed that 61% of crime victims did not believe that prison reduced reoffending for non-violent criminals. There was far more support for making offenders work in the community with 54% believing this would be more effective. A majority (51%) also favoured meetings between offenders and victims.

Only 28% of crime victims believed that prison was a suitable place to deal with drug-addicted offenders. When asked about long-term solutions, 72% said they wanted to see more drug treatment programmes in the community, and 66% wanted to see better provision for treating people with mental health problems. The results come as a book on criminal justice warns that government plans to develop the National Offender Management Service, integrating the prison and probation services, will backfire.

The authors say the plan would lead to a fragmented probation service that would have little impact on cutting reoffending rates.

Mike Hough of King's College London law school, one of the book's editors, said: 'The government is trying to move too far, too fast. They should concentrate on 'joining up' probation and prison work and avoid getting distracted by high-risk plans for structural reform.'

⇨ ICM interviewed a random sample of 982 adult victims of crime between 19 December 2005 and 7 January 2006.

16 January 2006

Victims of crime survey

ICM interviewed a random sample of 991 adults aged 18+, who have been a victim of crime, by telephone between 19 December 2005 and 8 January 2006. Interviews were conducted across the country and the results have been weighted to the profile of all adults.

Have you ever been a victim of crime? (Base: 3039)

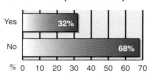

- Yes: 32%
- No: 68%

Did this crime take place within the past two year?

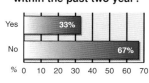

- Yes: 33%
- No: 67%

In your opinion, does the use of prison reduce reoffending for these types of crime?

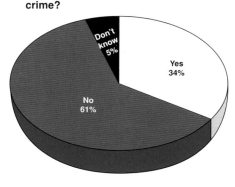

- Don't know 5%
- Yes 34%
- No 61%

In your opinion how well do you think the criminal justice system (e.g. Police, Crown Prosecution Service, Court Service) takes account of victims' needs?

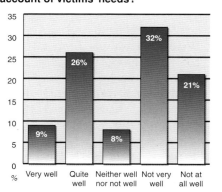

- Very well: 9%
- Quite well: 26%
- Neither well nor not well: 8%
- Not very well: 32%
- Not at all well: 21%

To what extent do you think the following are effective options for stopping offenders committing further crimes?

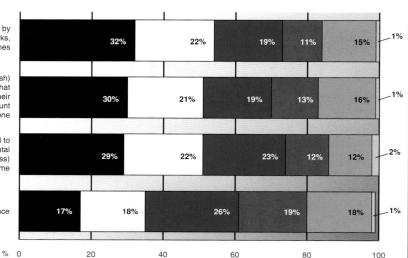

	Very effective	Quite effective	Neither effective nor not effective	Not very effective	Not at all effective	Don't know
Pay back to the community for the damage caused by doing compulsory work, for example in parks, schools and old people's homes	32%	22%	19%	11%	15%	1%
Meet their victims (if the victims wish) so victims can tell the offender what impact their behaviour had on them and their family and for the offender to be called to account and make amends for what they've done	30%	21%	19%	13%	16%	1%
Under probation supervision, offenders should be required to address the problems (e.g. drug addiction, mental illness, lack of education, homelessness) which may lead them to commit a crime	29%	22%	23%	12%	12%	2%
Receive a short custodial sentence	17%	18%	26%	19%	18%	1%

Legend:
- ■ Very effective
- □ Quite effective
- Neither effective nor not effective
- Not very effective
- Not at all effective
- Don't know

To what extent do you believe the following actions will be effective in reducing crime in the long run?

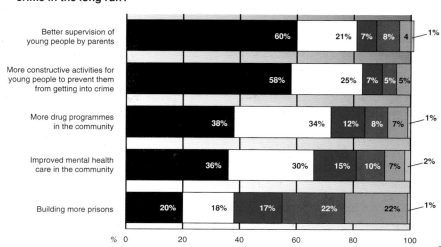

Better supervision of young people by parents	60%	21%	7%	8%	4	1%
More constructive activities for young people to prevent them from getting into crime	58%	25%	7%	5%	5%	
More drug programmes in the community	38%	34%	12%	8%	7%	1%
Improved mental health care in the community	36%	30%	15%	10%	7%	2%
Building more prisons	20%	18%	17%	22%	22%	1%

Source: ICM Research 2006 (www.icmresearch.co.uk)

Youth crime

Information from the Centre for Crime and Justice Studies

Youth crime in England and Wales has always been a controversial topic and very often appears in the media. Terms like 'yob' and 'ASBO' grab the headlines, but what are the crimes and who are the young people behind what's really going on? Are the behaviours of many children criminal, or sometimes are kids just being kids? Also, should young offenders be treated very differently or similarly to adult offenders?

The basics

⇨ A child in England and Wales is defined by law as anyone under the age of 18, while a young offender is someone who has been convicted of an offence between the age of 10 and 20.

⇨ Youth courts are specialist magistrates' courts that handle all but the most serious charges against people aged at least ten and under 18.

Should such young offenders be locked away? Why do young people commit crimes in the first place?

Youth justice facts in England and Wales

⇨ The age at which a child can be responsible for criminal behaviour in the England and Wales is 10 – one of the lowest in Europe.

⇨ The number of 15- to 17-year-olds in prison has more than doubled over the last ten years.

⇨ Statistics show that 287,013 offences were committed by 10- to 17-year-olds that resulted in convictions in 2004/05. This represents 20% of the 1.4 million such offences committed in that year.

The inside information on youth crime

How much youth crime is there?

⇨ It has been shown that the number of crimes committed by young people hasn't risen in the past five years,

and is decreasing over time. 'Crime' itself is something that is difficult to measure, but overall it seems that youth crime is going down.

⇨ Still, three-quarters of the public questioned in a survey said that they believed the number of young offenders had risen.

Possible measures

⇨ Almost half of 12- to 30-year-olds covered in a 1999 survey admitted committing at least one offence at some point in their lives (57% of men and 37% of women).

⇨ Still, the majority of crime is not committed by young people. In 2000, 88% of crime successfully dealt with by the police was committed by people over age 18, most of it by those over 21.

⇨ According to a 2004 survey, the majority of young people aged from 10 to 25 (74%) said they had not committed any of 20 offences (such as theft, assault, and selling drugs) listed.

Reoffending rates

A big concern with young offenders (and also with adult offenders) is that they may commit more crimes even after they are punished for previous ones. The statistics show that this is likely to happen especially if a young person has been put into custody for their behaviour.

⇨ 73% of young offenders aged 18 to 21 and 82% of young males aged 15 to 18 are reconvicted within two years of release from custody.

⇨ Older child offenders have higher reoffending rates than younger child offenders.

⇨ In one survey, eight per cent of all young people aged from 10 to 25 admitted to committing an offence six or more times in the last 12

months. They are therefore called 'frequent offenders'.

So what can help stop children from reoffending? Rehabilitation, family support, assistance with finding a place to live, and securing a job after custody are all likely to help. As the numbers show, 'punishment' alone such as jail time doesn't seem to make young people stop committing crimes.

How serious is youth crime?

Most of what we hear about young people and crime in the media involves anti-social behaviour, violence, and sometimes even just kids hanging out in large groups on the street. Is all of this behaviour criminal? No, but when crimes do take place, how serious are they?

⇨ Theft, handling stolen goods, burglary, fraud or forgery and criminal damage make up more than 68% of youth crime.

⇨ Almost eight in ten of the incidents self-reported in a 2004 survey were not of a serious nature. The most common offences were non-injury assaults (28%); the selling of non-Class A substances (19%) and thefts from the workplace or from school (16%).

⇨ When violent incidents do occur, many don't involve injury and are often committed on the 'spur of the moment' against someone the young person knows. This often means a fight (maybe between friends) and usually takes place near home in the afternoon time.

⇨ At the end of December 2005 more children were in prison for robbery than any other offence.

⇨ Despite media attention on violent offending, few cautions or convictions relate to violence.

How is youth crime dealt with?

Possible outcomes

So what happens when a young person has been caught committing a crime? Below is a list of possible outcomes for dealing with child offenders. Some seem very serious while others may only involve a warning:

⇨ Reprimand: A formal verbal warning given for a minor first offence, after which the young person may be referred to a Youth Offending Team (YOT).
⇨ Final warning: A formal verbal warning given for a first or second offence, after which the young person is given a programme of activities identified to address the causes of their offending behaviour.
⇨ Custody: Formal detention such as through a Detention and Training Order (DTO).
⇨ Community Sentences: These include non-custody options such as Supervision or Reparation Orders.
⇨ Anti-Social Behaviour Order: Often referred to as an ASBO.
⇨ Curfew Order: Requires the offender to remain in a certain place (usually their home) for certain times of the day.
⇨ Parenting Order: Can impose a requirement on the parent or guardian to attend counselling or guidance sessions.
⇨ Drug Treatment and Testing Order: The young person receives regular drug testing and treatment in the community, and is supervised by the Probation Service.
⇨ Child Safety Orders: Places a child under ten who is at risk of becoming involved in offending, or is behaving in an anti-social manner, under supervision.
⇨ Intensive Supervision and Surveillance Programmes (ISSP): Places the young offender under supervision and surveillance of a YOT usually for six months. This can involve being monitored for 25 hours a week.

Please see the CCJS factsheet 'Young People in Prison' for more information on custodial accommodation types and statistics.

Restorative justice/ conferencing

Restorative justice usually involves a conference, or meeting, where the offender sits down with the victim, family members, and possibly other people from the community or people related to the crime.

⇨ This means that they do not have to make a court appearance.
⇨ The purpose of the meeting is to discuss the offending behaviour and come up with ways for the young person to 'repay' the victim or community for their crime.

An ASBO is a civil order against behaviour which causes 'alarm, harassment or distress'

⇨ This repayment may be in the form of an apology letter or some volunteer work for example.

But what about ASBOs?

ASBO stands for Anti-Social Behaviour Order, and is a very controversial idea. Although the government claims that the use of ASBOs is not aimed at young people, they bring many children into the criminal justice system who haven't actually committed any crimes.

⇨ An ASBO is a civil order against behaviour which causes 'alarm, harassment or distress'. These are pretty vague words and can cover things such as graffiti, truancy from school, shoplifting, or even just playing loud music.
⇨ Non-compliance is a criminal matter, meaning individuals can be jailed for up to five years if they break the ASBO rules. This means children can end up in jail for offences that would not put them there in the first place – such as playing loud music.
⇨ Alarmingly, breaking the rules of an ASBO is estimated to happen frequently.
⇨ There were 7,356 ASBOs issued from 1999 through 2005. Of these, 43.8% were issued to 10- to 17-year-olds, and 56.2% to over-18s.
⇨ People who do not like the use of the ASBO system argue that

it criminalises behaviour that is otherwise lawful, and only punishes bad behaviour rather than helping to improve it.

How serious is anti-social behaviour then? It can be hard to define what is considered anti-social activity, and what may be just everyday activity for a lot of kids.

⇨ The most common type of anti-social behaviour is being noisy or rude in public.
⇨ Speeding traffic is the most commonly mentioned 'problem behaviour' according to 43% of people in a recent survey.

Other interventions also target young people who are deemed 'at risk' of offending before they actually commit any crimes:

⇨ Youth Inclusion Programmes (YIPs): Target to support the 50 most at risk 13- to 16-year-olds in high crime areas and operate in 72 of the most deprived and high crime areas in England and Wales.
⇨ Youth Inclusion and Support Panels (YISPs): Are in 92 areas identified most at risk for 7- to 13-year-olds, providing programmes of support with the view to prevent offending.

Who's in charge?

The Youth Justice Board

The Youth Justice Board (YJB) is a non-departmental public body sponsored by the Home Office which oversees the youth justice system in England and Wales.

⇨ It advises the Home Secretary on the operation of, and standards for, the youth justice system.
⇨ The YJB helps find young offenders places to live if necessary.

What's a YOT?

A Youth Offending Team (YOT) is a team which was set up after the 1998 Crime and Disorder Act, to provide counsel and rehabilitation to offenders.

⇨ YOTs carry out a variety of work with young offenders and include people from areas such as the Police Service, Probation Service, Social Services, the Health Service, Education and Psychology.
⇨ The goal of a YOT is to identify the needs of individual young offenders by looking at problems specific to them.

The age of criminal responsibility: an ongoing debate

How old does a child have to be before they can be found guilty of committing a crime? In England and Wales the age of criminal responsibility is 10- lower than in many other countries. Children under the age of 10 lack capacity to commit a crime. The legal term for this rule is *doli incapax*.

⇨ Until 1998, *doli incapax* meant that the age of criminal responsibility used to be 14.

⇨ This changed in the 1998 Crime and Disorder Act, meaning that children between the ages of 10 and 14 are now presumed capable of committing a crime.

Photo: Sara Hoffman

⇨ Since 1998, there has been an increase in young offenders going to court even though they may not understand the consequences of what they've done.

⇨ It has been recently suggested that the age of criminal responsibility should be raised from 10 back to 14 to make sure that children are treated differently than adults in the justice system.

⇨ Compare the age of 10 with other countries' age of criminal responsibility:
  ↳ Canada: 12
  ↳ France: 13
  ↳ Germany: 14
  ↳ Japan: 14
  ↳ Russia: 14
  ↳ Italy: 15
  ↳ Norway: 15
  ↳ Spain: 16
  ↳ Belgium: 18
  ↳ Luxembourg: 18.

So why is it so low in England and Wales?

A note about the Bulger case

James Bulger was a two-year-old boy who was murdered by two 10-year-old boys, in England in 1993.

⇨ The murder of a child by two other children caused shock and public outrage, and after the trial the two boys were ordered to serve a minimum of 10 years behind bars.

⇨ This murder, due to the violence involved and the young age of the offenders, undoubtedly influenced the decision to change the age of criminal responsibility in 1998 by the New Labour Government.

Is the youth justice system succeeding?

Many people may agree that the youth justice system has taken some steps in the right direction by making more alternatives to custody available with different orders and community sentences. Still, the numbers of young people locked up remain high, and the task of addressing the causes of offending behaviour isn't straightforward.

Causes of youth crime

Why do young people commit crimes in the first place? Of course there is no easy answer, but it is more helpful to look at background experiences and life situations, than to just focus on punishments for behaviour. Some key risk factors identified for youth offending are:

⇨ being male
⇨ having a parent or parents who are offenders
⇨ not living with parents/ being in care
⇨ suffering bereavement or family breakdown
⇨ drug or alcohol misuse
⇨ experiencing neglect, physical, sexual or emotional abuse
⇨ witnessing violence against a family member
⇨ playing truant or being excluded from school
⇨ associating with delinquent friends
⇨ having siblings or other family members who offend.

So what does this list say about how young offenders should be dealt with? Activists claim that being locked up certainly doesn't resolve any of these risk factors.

Youth crime and education

A lot of young people who end up in custody have had very bad experiences with education, or were excluded from school.

⇨ Looking at the youngest children in custody showed that out of 23 children, only one was in mainstream education.

⇨ The Prison Inspectorate's report on young people's perceptions of prison found that 83% of boys in Young Offenders Institutes had been excluded from school at some time in the past, and that 2 in 5 said they had played truant every day.

Youth crime and mental health

Mental health problems can play a big part in offending for young people and must be addressed. Putting children with mental health problems in jail or giving them ASBOs and other orders can be especially damaging to them.

⇨ Examples of mental health problems include learning disabilities, ADHD, and autism.

⇨ Children from poorer backgrounds, children in care and those who have witnessed domestic violence, are all at particular risk of developing mental health problems.

⇨ One study found that 35% of young people with ASBOs had a diagnosed mental disorder or learning difficulty.

The country of Finland has tiny numbers of young people locked up but places many children in special psychiatric units because of mental health concerns. This sort of concern and focus on mental health and well-being is very different from England and Wales.

Youth crime and victimisation

Many young offenders are not only offenders, they are victims too. Being a victim makes many children more likely to commit crimes themselves.

⇨ Young men, aged 16 to 24, were most at risk of being a victim of violent crime; 14.6% experienced a violent crime of some sort in the year prior to their British Crime Survey interview in 2004/05.

⇨ Risk factors from a 2004 survey show that just over half (52%) of those who admitted offending in the last year had also been a victim, compared with 23% of non-offenders.

⇨ The above information is reprinted with kind permission from the Centre for Crime and Justice Studies. Visit www.crimeinfo.org.uk for more information.

© CCJS

Young offenders, policing and prisons in the UK

Information from the Economic and Social Research Council

This information provides a statistical overview of young offenders, policing and prisons. It is designed to introduce the topic rather than be a comprehensive summary.

The extent of youth crime

Surveys show that offending of some kind is common among young people. In the Youth Lifestyles Survey of 12- to 30-year-olds, almost half (57 per cent of males and 37 per cent females) admitted committing at least one of 27 offences at some point in their lives. These included arson, theft, shoplifting, violent offences and fraud.

The Peterborough Youth Study (an ESRC-funded project) showed that 38 per cent of its 1,957 sample of 14 to 15-year-old adolescents had committed offences such as arson, vandalism, theft and burglary.

However, the number of young offenders actually cautioned or convicted is proportionately much less.

Prevalence of and type of offences

The Youth Lifestyles Survey found that the average age at which offending began was 13.5 for boys and 14 for girls. Among those aged 12 to 13, a similar proportion of boys and girls had offended. However, by the time they reached 17, male offenders outnumbered women offenders by a ratio of about 3:1. Offending for both sexes generally declines after the age of 21.

One in five of male crimes are violent, whereas this is only one in ten for females.

In a national survey of problem behaviour among young people, one in ten 11-year-old boys and almost a quarter of 16-year-olds said they had carried a weapon in the past year. One in five 16-year-old boys admitted attacking someone intending to hurt them seriously.

In the Youth Lifestyles Survey of 12- to 30-year-olds, almost half (57 per cent of males and 37 per cent females) admitted committing at least one of 27 offences at some point in their lives

---

Under-age drinking was also common. More than four out of ten students in Year 10 (14- to 15-year-olds) and over half in Year 11 acknowledged 'binges', where they consumed five or more alcoholic drinks in a session. Three out of ten boys and one in four girls in Year 11 (15- to 16-year-olds) said they had used cannabis at least once. Use of more harmful illegal drugs was much lower.

Pathways into crime

The Edinburgh Study of Youth Transitions and Crime have found a very strong link between being a victim of crime and breaking the law. At age 15, offending was seven times higher for young people who had themselves been victims of five types of crime, than it was for 15-year-olds who had not been victims of any crimes. The link was even stronger if the young person had been robbed or assaulted with a weapon.

Youth's routines and lifestyle are strong predictors of offending. Adolescents who spend a high degree of their time with their peers and a low degree of their time with their family tend to be more involved in offending than others.

Policing

Boys are more likely than girls to report having negative contact with the police for the first time at age 12 or under. However, most young people had a good opinion of the police with two-thirds of 12- to 30-year-olds feeling that the police do a very, or fairly, good job. The same proportion said that they would feel safer if there were more police patrolling the streets on foot.

In 2004/05, victims were very or fairly satisfied with the way the police handled the matter in 58 per cent of the incidents that the police came to know about. This remains stable compared with 2003/04 (58%) and also 2002/03 (59%).

Juveniles in prison

In April 2004, there were over 2,800 young people in custody. Of these only 138 were female. Over 80 per cent of boys had been excluded from school and 43 per cent of girls had been in care or foster-homes.

One in six boys and girls reported having an alcohol problem on arrival in prison, and 40 per cent admitted to a drug problem. 91 per cent of girls and 89 per cent of boys wanted to stop offending; they believed that finding a job was the thing most likely to prevent reoffending. 32 per cent of boys and 44 per cent of girls felt that they had done something in custody that would help find a job, but nearly a third of those about to be released still needed help with resettlement problems.

Repeat offenders

According to the Criminal Justice System, 36.9 per cent of juveniles (10 to 17 years old) who were convicted of crimes in the first three months of 2003 were reconvicted within one year. The graph below ('Reconviction rates by sexes') also shows that this rate is lower for female offenders.

The table below ('Risk factors for persistent offending in last year [males]') shows the factors most strongly associated with persistent offending. Using drugs in the last year was the strongest predictor, with the odds of offending nearly five times higher for boys who had used drugs compared with those who had not. However, preliminary results from more recent research suggest that although drug use tends to increase with age, this is not associated with an increase in offending.

Pathways out of crime

A major study of crime in Chicago found that while a high level of poverty and racial segregation is generally associated with delinquency, crime and violence, this is reduced in areas where neighbours co-operate, meet, and work together to get things done and intervene on behalf of the common good.

Data on crime

The Economic and Social Data Service produces a detailed guide to quality data resources for researchers investigating crime. It is available at http://www.esds.ac.uk/qualidata/access/criminology.asp

---

One in six boys and girls reported having an alcohol problem on arrival in prison, and 40 per cent admitted to a drug problem

---

⇨ The above information is reprinted with kind permission from the Economic and Social Research Council. Visit www.esrc.ac.uk for more information.

© ESRC

Offending in the UK

Volume of offences by 12- to 30-year-olds.

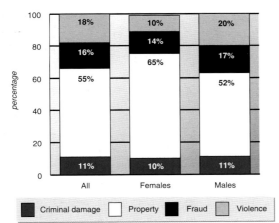

Source: Youth Crime: Findings from the 1998/1999 Youth Lifestyles Survey, Home Office. Available at: http://www.homeoffice.gov.uk/rds/pdfs/hors209.pdf. This survey was based on a sample of 4,848 people aged between 12 and 30 in England and Wales. Taken from the ESRC factsheet 'Young Offenders, Policing and Prisons in the UK'.

Reconviction rates by sexes.

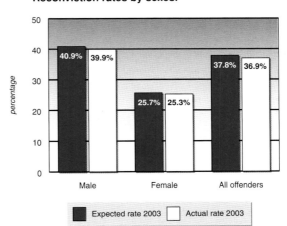

Juvenile reconviction: results from the 2003 cohort published by the Home Office and available at http://www.homeoffice.gov.uk/rds/crimeew0405.html. Crown copyright. Taken from the ESRC factsheet 'Young Offenders, Policing and Prisons in the UK'.

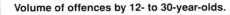

Risk factors for persistent offending in last year (males)									
	Used drugs in last year	Used drugs at least once a month	Drinks at least five times a week	Disaffected from school	Truanted from school at least once a month	Temporary or permanent exclusion from school	No qualifications on leaving school	Delinquent friends or acquaintances	Parents rarely or never know whereabouts	Hangs around in public
12- to 17-year-olds	✔			✔	✔			✔	✔	✔
18- to 30-year-olds		✔	✔			✔	✔	✔		

Source: Youth Crime: Findings from the 1998/1999 Youth Lifestyles Survey, Home Office. Available at: http://www.homeoffice.gov.uk/rds/pdfs/hors209.pdf. This survey was based on a sample of 4,848 people aged between 12 and 30 in England and Wales. Taken from the ESRC factsheet 'Young Offenders, Policing and Prisons in the UK'.

Young people and crime

Findings from the 2005 Offending, Crime and Justice Survey – a summary

This report presents the first findings from the 2005 Offending, Crime and Justice Survey (OCJS). It focuses on levels and trends in youth offending, anti-social behaviour and victimisation among young people aged from 10 to 25 living in the general household population in England and Wales. The survey does not cover young people living in institutions, including prisons, or the homeless, and thus omits some high offending groups.

Extent of offending – Chapter 2

Chapter 2 provides an overview of the extent of offending in those crimes covered by the survey and the proportion of young people who have committed these offences in the last 12 months. In addition, it examines levels of serious and frequent offending, identifies the proportion of crime accounted for by frequent offenders, and the proportion of young people who in the last 12 months have committed other offences covered in the survey, e.g. carried weapons (knives or guns), handling stolen goods and racially/religiously motivated assaults.

⇨ Three-quarters (75%) of young people had not offended in the last 12 months. Of the 25 per cent that committed at least one of the offences in the last 12 months, many had offended only occasionally or committed relatively trivial offences. The proportion of young people committing an offence remained stable across all three waves of the survey. This pattern held for frequent and serious offenders.

⇨ The most commonly reported offence categories were assault (committed by 16%) and other thefts (11%). Criminal damage, drug selling offences and vehicle-related thefts were less common and burglary and robbery were relatively rare at one per cent or less.

⇨ Males were more likely to have offended in the last 12 months than females (30% compared to 21% respectively). For males the prevalence of offending peaked among 16- to 19-year-olds, whilst for females the prevalence peaked earlier at age 14 to 15.

⇨ Seven per cent of all young people were classified as frequent offenders, i.e. they had committed an offence six or more times in the last 12 months. This group was responsible for the vast majority (83%) of all offences measured in the survey.

⇨ Thirteen per cent of all 10- to 25-year-olds had committed at least one of the serious offences measured. The majority (71%) of serious offenders had committed an assault resulting in injury and no other serious offence. One per cent of all 10- to 25-year-olds had frequently committed serious offences (i.e. committed serious offences six or more time in the last 12 months) and were classified as frequent serious offenders.

⇨ The proportion of 10- to 25-year-olds who said they had physically attacked someone because of their skin colour, race or religion (racially/religiously motivated assault) in the last 12 months was relatively low, at less than one per cent. The level of racially/religiously motivated assaults has remained stable between the 2004 and 2005 waves of the survey.

⇨ Overall, four per cent of young people had carried a knife in the last 12 months. Males were significantly more likely than females to have carried a knife (5% versus 2%). Of the four per cent that had carried a knife, over eight in ten (85%) said the reason for doing so was for protection and nine per cent said it was in case they got into a fight.

⇨ One-fifth (20%) of 12- to 25-year-olds had handled (bought or sold) stolen goods in the last 12 months. Seven per cent had sold stolen goods and 19 per cent had bought stolen goods. The levels of handling stolen goods for 12- to 25-year-olds have remained stable between 2004 and 2005. This pattern held for both selling and buying stolen goods.

Characteristics of offenders – Chapter 3

Risk factors associated with offending (including serious and frequent offenders) for different age groups are presented in this chapter.

In addition it examines the overlaps of committing offences and anti-social behaviour; offending and drug use; and offending and personal victimisation.

⇨ For 10- to 15-year-olds the particular attributes that were independently statistically associated and showed the strongest association with committing an offence were: committing anti-social behaviour; being a victim of personal crime; being drunk once a month or more; having friends/siblings in trouble with the police; and taking drugs. Similar factors were found for serious and frequent offending.

⇨ For 16- to 25-year-olds the particular attributes that were independently statistically associated and showed the strongest association with committing an offence were: being a victim of personal crime; committing anti-social behaviour; taking drugs; having friends/siblings in trouble with the police; and being more likely to agree criminal acts are OK. Again for frequent and serious offending, similar factors were found to be strongly associated.

Contact with the criminal justice system – Chapter 4

This chapter focuses on the extent to which offenders and offences are dealt with by the police and the courts.

It is well established that the proportion of offences that result in a criminal justice sanction is low. Some offences may never become known to anyone and of those that are known about not all are reported to the police. Furthermore, many offences that are known to the police do not result in the offender being detected.

⇨ In the last 12 months, four per cent of all 10- to 25-year-olds had been arrested, two per cent had been to court accused of committing a criminal offence and one per cent had been given a community/custodial sentence or fine. The general levels of contact with the criminal justice system were similar between the survey waves (there were no significant changes).

⇨ Young people who committed an offence in the last 12 months were significantly more likely than those who had not offended in the last 12 months to have been arrested, taken to court or have been given a fine, community or custodial sentence. Just under one in ten (8%) of those who said they had offended in the last 12 months reported that they had been arrested in the same period, while one in twenty offenders (5%) had been to court.

⇨ 13 per cent of young people who had offended in the last year said the police had spoken to them about at least one of the offences they had committed in the last 12 months, although not necessarily

arrested them. Three per cent said they had appeared in court or were due to appear in court, and two per cent had been convicted of an offence.

⇨ Violent offences were the offences most likely to result in the respondent having contact with the police.

Anti-social and other problem behaviours – Chapter 5

Levels of anti-social behaviour and other problem behaviours are presented including associated risk factors. Anti-social behaviour as measured by the OCJS covers: being noisy or rude in a public place so that people complained or the individual got into trouble with the police; behaving in a way that resulted in a neighbour complaining; graffiti in a public place; threatening or being rude to someone because of their race or religion.

⇨ Over three-quarters (77%) of young people had not committed at least one of the four anti-social behaviours in the last 12 months. Of the 23 per cent who had committed anti-social behaviour, most had only done so once or twice.

⇨ The proportions of young people committing each of the four anti-social behaviours, and the proportion committing at least one, were stable across the three waves of the survey. This was true for both males and females and for both 10- to 17-year-olds and 18- to 25- year-olds.

⇨ Similar to offending, males were significantly more likely than females to have committed anti-social behaviour in the last 12 months; 10- to 17-year-olds were more likely than 18- to 25-year-olds to have committed anti-social behaviour.

⇨ For both age groups (10- to 15-year-olds and 16- to 25-year-olds) the factors that were independently strongly associated with committing anti-social behaviour were: committing an offence; having friends/siblings in trouble with the police; and taking any drug. For 10- to 15-year-olds, perceiving their parents to have poor parenting skills was

also strongly associated, while for 16- to 25-year-olds, being highly impulsive was strongly associated. These results are similar to those found for offending.

Personal victimisation – Chapter 6

The extent and nature of personal victimisation among young people are presented in this chapter together with the associated risk factors. Crimes included in the definition of personal victimisation are robbery, theft from the person, other personal thefts, assault with injury and assault without injury.

⇨ Just over a quarter (27%) of young people had been the victim of personal crime in the last 12 months. The most common forms of victimisation were assault without injury (11%) and other personal thefts (9%). Overall levels of victimisation remained stable across the three waves of the survey.

⇨ 10- to 15-year-olds were more likely than 16- to 25-year-olds to have been victims of personal crime in the last 12 months. However, the majority of incidents against 10- to 15- year-olds happened at school, perpetrated by pupils or friends and seen by the victims as 'something that happens' and 'wrong but not a crime'. The most common forms of victimisation for both age groups (10- to 15-year-olds and 16- to 25-year-olds) were assault without injury (11%) and other personal thefts (9%).

⇨ For 10- to 15-year-olds the factors most strongly independently associated with being a victim of personal crime were: committing an offence, being male and identifying one or more disorder problem in their area. For 16- to 25-year-olds committing an offence, having a negative attitude towards their local area and not trusting the police were the most strongly associated factors.
December 2006

⇨ The above information is reprinted with kind permission from the Home Office. Visit www.homeoffice.gov.uk for more information.

© Crown copyright

Statistics from the Ipsos MORI release 'Attitudes towards teenagers and crime', 24 April 2006. Respondents were asked the following:

Thinking now about the last occasion that you felt worried about groups of teenagers hanging around on the local streets, what were they actually doing that was causing a problem?

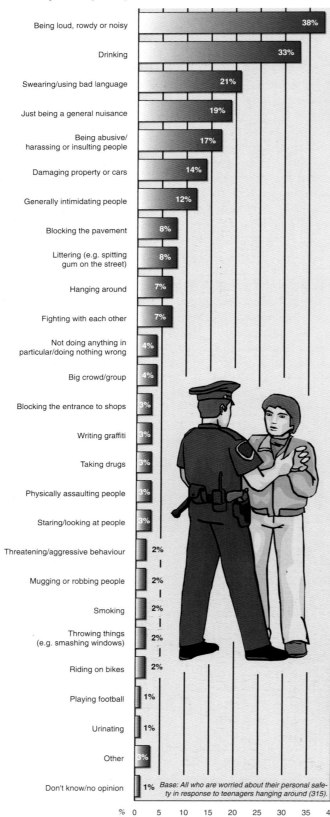

Being loud, rowdy or noisy	38%
Drinking	33%
Swearing/using bad language	21%
Just being a general nuisance	19%
Being abusive/harassing or insulting people	17%
Damaging property or cars	14%
Generally intimidating people	12%
Blocking the pavement	8%
Littering (e.g. spitting gum on the street)	8%
Hanging around	7%
Fighting with each other	7%
Not doing anything in particular/doing nothing wrong	4%
Big crowd/group	4%
Blocking the entrance to shops	3%
Writing graffiti	3%
Taking drugs	3%
Physically assaulting people	3%
Staring/looking at people	3%
Threatening/aggressive behaviour	2%
Mugging or robbing people	2%
Smoking	2%
Throwing things (e.g. smashing windows)	2%
Riding on bikes	2%
Playing football	1%
Urinating	1%
Other	3%
Don't know/no opinion	1%

Base: All who are worried about their personal safety in response to teenagers hanging around (315).

% 0 5 10 15 20 25 30 35 40

When you are out in your local area and you see groups of teenagers hanging around the streets, generally, how worried do you feel about your own personal safety?

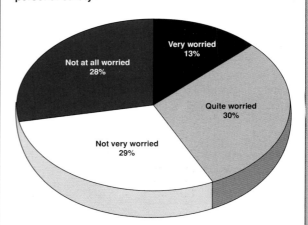

Very worried 13%
Quite worried 30%
Not very worried 29%
Not at all worried 28%

Base: All who have seen teenagers hanging around their local area (708)

Of every 100 crimes recorded by the police, how many do you think are committed by young offenders, that is people aged between 10 and 17?

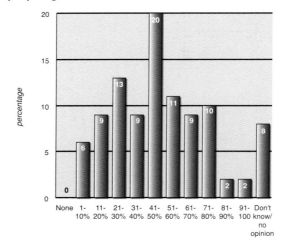

None	1-10%	11-20%	21-30%	31-40%	41-50%	51-60%	61-70%	71-80%	81-90%	91-100%	Don't know/no opinion
0	6	9	13	9	20	11	9	10	2	2	8

percentage

Do you think that the number of young offenders (that is people aged between 10 and 17) has increased, decreased, or stayed the same over the past two years?

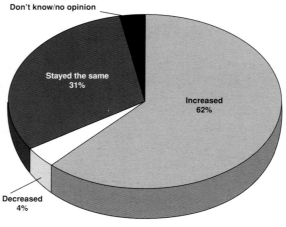

Don't know/no opinion
Stayed the same 31%
Increased 62%
Decreased 4%

Base: 1,001 adults aged 18+, UK. Source: Ipsos MORI, March 2006.

Crisis in custody

Crisis point reached as the number of young people in custody reaches record high

A crisis is facing children and young people in custody, as the number of under-18s held in secure accommodation in England and Wales reaches a record high.

The stark warning, from YJB Chairman, Rod Morgan, HM Chief Inspector of Prisons, Anne Owers, and the Children's Commissioner for England, Professor Sir Albert Aynsley-Green, came today during a visit to Feltham Young Offender Institution in west London.

The number of under-18s held in secure accommodation in England and Wales reaches a record high

'Over 3,350 children and young people are being held today in custody. The youth justice system has just a handful of bed spaces left,' said Professor Morgan. 'We can't simply put up a sign saying "No Vacancies". Action is urgently needed to stop custody for young people going into meltdown.'

While praising the excellent work undertaken at Feltham in difficult circumstances, Morgan, Owers and Aynsley-Green called for an honest debate into alternative ways to deal with young offenders who commit low level and less serious crimes.

'Of course the public must be protected from serious, persistent and prolific offenders. But we believe custody should be used only as a last resort. As a start, we are calling on

A crisis is facing children and young people in custody, as the number of under-18s held in secure accommodation

the Government and sentencers to make better use of intensive supervision community sentences, which can play a major role in reducing reoffending.'

The rise in custodial population is causing a range of serious problems including:
⇨ an increased risk of self-harm and suicide by vulnerable young people in custody, including those who have mental health problems
⇨ difficulties in running education, vocational and crime reduction courses that can help young people stay out of trouble on their release
⇨ the 'bussing' of young people around the country, making it difficult for family contact to be maintained

⇨ an increased risk of major disturbances and indiscipline by young people as hard-pressed staff struggle to maintain order
⇨ increased sharing of cells.

Feltham YOI, west London, continues to ensure the safety of all young people within its establishment and provides sound educational and vocational services for its young people – designed to equip them with the necessary skills to help them gain entry into further education and jobs.

Chief Inspector of Prisons, Anne Owers, said: 'Every time I go into a custodial establishment, I see staff achieving amazing things in difficult circumstances with highly troubled young people. But I fear the system is approaching breaking point. And I am particularly concerned about the number of young people with mental illness who end up in our prisons because of the lack of adequate provision outside'

The Children's Commissioner for England, Professor Sir Albert Aynsley-Green, said: 'Custody is not effective in preventing crime. It is costly and does enormous damage to children who are, for the most part, already extremely vulnerable. It fails to offer children the support they need to rehabilitate and change their behaviour. In line with the recommendations of the UN Convention on the Rights of the Child, custody for children and young people should be used only as a last resort, and then only for the small numbers who are a risk to themselves or others. Shutting children away in prison sends a message that we are giving up on them. If progress is to be made, we need to tackle the root causes of crime.'
24 October 2006

⇨ Information from the Youth Justice Board. Visit www.yjb.gov.uk for more information.

Teen gangs

Streetwise teens gang together to avoid trouble and stay safe

Groups of teenagers 'hanging out' on the streets may look intimidating, but young people often gang together with friends as a way of keeping safe and avoiding trouble, according to a study of parents and children in disadvantaged communities for the Joseph Rowntree Foundation.

The research with families in four neighbourhoods of Glasgow found that young people pooled their detailed local knowledge to avoid hazards, including violence from more organised gangs and aggression from adults with drink and drug problems. They took responsibility for keeping themselves and friends safe by moving around in groups and looking out for each other, using mobile phones to stay in touch.

> **Groups of teenagers 'hanging out' on the streets may look intimidating, but young people often gang together with friends as a way of keeping safe**

'We were impressed by the positive part that young people's peer groups played in helping them to stay safe,' said Prof. Malcolm Hill, Director of the Glasgow Centre for the Child and Society, who led the research project on children's resilience. 'Parents were generally unaware of its importance and young people themselves recognised that sticking together in groups could, in spite of their self-protective intentions, appear threatening to some adults.'

He added: 'Both parents and children in these deprived neighbourhoods were keenly aware of risks within their communities and the young people had often become experts in avoiding potential trouble. They knew about avoiding people, places and certain times of day, and they deployed a range of other strategies, including keeping a low profile or asking friends or parents to accompany them in order to keep safe.'

The study, which combined questionnaire surveys of 'ordinary' families with in-depth interviews, found that parents and children usually identified positive aspects of their neighbourhoods, in spite of high levels of unemployment, low income and drug misuse. These positive aspects were often associated with family, friends and neighbours.

It also highlighted a strong commitment among parents to protect children from the worst effects of low income and to keep them safe from local dangers.

This sometimes meant placing restrictions on children's movements and activities, including visits to local amenities such as parks and sports facilities. Children were mostly accepting of rules about time and place, which they took as a sign of their parents' concern. However, as they grew older some young people kept quiet about certain activities, believing they could take care of themselves.

The report calls on national and local policy makers to build on the strengths and aspirations of parents and children in disadvantaged areas, as well as tackling the heightened risks they face, such as drug misuse and antisocial behaviour. For example, policies could do more to support the informal local networks that share information about safe activities and provide families with practical advice and support.

Schools are also urged to capitalise on the evidence of parents' positive commitment to discipline and their children's safety to engage them as allies in strategies to raise standards of behaviour.

Peter Seaman, co-author of the report, said: 'Parenting has been prominent in many government policies, including initiatives to tackle crime, and there is a widespread view that antisocial and delinquent behaviour by young people can simply be blamed on "bad" parenting. Yet the parents we interviewed described sophisticated strategies they had adopted to minimise their children's exposure to danger and to guard them against temptations to go "off the rails".

'They also had high aspirations for their children, wanting them to have better opportunities in life than they had experienced. What appeared to be lacking was the capacity to fulfil the hopes they held, especially in education, because they did not have the knowledge or resources to realise them.'

Note

Parenting and children's resilience in disadvantaged communities by Peter Seaman, Katrina Turner, Malcolm Hill, Anne Stafford and Moira Walker, is published for the Foundation by the National Children's Bureau, 8 Wakley Street, London EC1V 7QE (020 7843 6000) price £13.95, plus £3 p&p.
20 February 2006

⇨ The above information is reprinted with kind permission from the Joseph Rowntree Foundation. Please visit www.jrf.org.uk for more information.

© *Joseph Rowntree Foundation*

ASBOs

It's a word that's always being bandied around in the papers, but where does it come from and how could you be affected?

The Anti-Social Behaviour Act

In January 2004, then Home Secretary David Blunkett's Anti-Social Behaviour Act came into force introducing a whole lot of new laws affecting young people. Here is a short summary of the laws that will affect you.

⇨ Carrying air guns in public 'without lawful authority or excuse' has been criminalised so it is now an arrestable offence;

⇨ The age for legal possession of air weapons has been raised from 14 to 17;

The Government brought in the ASBO in the Crime and Disorder Act 1998. Getting one doesn't give you a criminal record, but if you breach the terms of the ASBO, it's a criminal offence

---

⇨ On-the-spot fines for offences such as throwing fireworks and making hoax 999 calls have been extended from adults only to 16- and 17-year-olds;

⇨ Newspapers and local councils can name youngsters punished with anti-social behaviour orders;

⇨ Police get the power to close crack dens in 48 hours and keep them closed, getting over a loophole that used to allow the dens to reopen with new dealers;

⇨ Accredited private security firms have police powers to issue £30 on-the-spot fines to cyclists for riding on the pavement;

⇨ These street wardens can also fine people found drunk and disorderly in a public place £40 if aged 16 or over, and fine anyone caught buying alcohol for someone under 18 £40 (again if aged 16 or over);

⇨ The Act gives police the power to disperse large groups of young people who have gathered in an area designated an anti-social behaviour hotspot by a local council.

Why the controversy?

The new Act has provoked much debate in the media, the main concerns being:

⇨ Some children's charities believe the Act will victimise innocent young people;

⇨ Equal rights groups suggest that it will unfairly target ethnic minorities.

ASBOs (Anti-Social Behaviour Orders)

The Government brought in the ASBO in the Crime and Disorder Act 1998. Getting one doesn't give you a criminal record, but if you breach the terms of the ASBO, it's a criminal offence.

ASBOs can be used on any person over the age of 10 and can last up to two years. You may be at risk of getting one if you do one of the following:

⇨ Graffiti;

⇨ Abusive and intimidating language, often directed at minorities;

⇨ Excessive noise, particularly late at night;

⇨ Fouling the street with litter;

⇨ Drunken behaviour in the streets, and the mess it creates;

⇨ Dealing drugs;

⇨ Harassment of residents or passers-by;

⇨ Verbal abuse;

⇨ Criminal damage;

⇨ Vandalism;

⇨ Engaging in threatening behaviour in large groups;

⇨ Racial abuse;

⇨ Smoking or drinking alcohol while under age;

⇨ Substance misuse;

⇨ Joyriding;

⇨ Begging;

⇨ Prostitution;

⇨ Kerb-crawling;

⇨ Throwing missiles;

⇨ Assault;

⇨ Vehicle crime.

⇨ The above information is reprinted with kind permission from TheSite.org. Visit www.thesite.org for more information.

© TheSite.org

High levels of support for ASBOs

To what extent do you support or oppose the issuing of ASBOs to people responsible for anti-social behaviour?

- Strongly oppose 1%
- Tend to oppose 3%
- Don't know 2%
- Neither/nor 12%
- Strongly support 42%
- Tend to support 40%

Base: All respondents in England and Wales (1,857)

Source: Ipsos MORI, May 2005.

ASBO mania

Are ASBOs working or are young people being failed by the system?

If you don't know what ASBO stands for, then you've probably been living on another planet for the last year. For those of you who have just arrived back on earth, ASBO is the government's new buzz acronym, standing for 'Anti-Social Behaviour Order'.

ASBOs have caused as much controversy as they have confusion and here Charlotte Lytton, from Children's Express, explores whether ASBOs are working or whether young people are being failed by the system.

The subject of ASBOs has become one of great controversy. Over 4,483 of them have been given out in the past five and a half years. But are they really having any impact on the youth of today who are committing crimes, or are they doing more harm to them than good?

ASBOs were introduced in April 1999, aimed at tackling relentless low level street crime. However, 42% of ASBOs issued were breached in their first two and a half years. Statistics like this have become an increasing cause for concern for many people who feel they're not worth the paper they're written on. Criminal Defence solicitor and ASBO concern national co-ordinator Matt Foot says the government are dreaming if they think ASBOs are working.

But what about the ordinary person on the street? What do they think? 15-year-old Ginisha from London says: 'They're not really working, so what's the point?' And it's not just young people who think this. But do ordinary people on the streets of London agree? I went to find out. Roland, 42, says, 'They're not a good idea. It's just a silly little knee-jerk reaction to something that desperately needs a wider response.'

Over 4,483 [ASBOs] have been given out in the past five and a half years

But it's not just members of the public who have a problem with ASBOs. It's not uncommon to see sketches about them on TV shows like the immensely popular *Little Britain* where character Vicky Pollard boasts about the number of times she's been in trouble with the police.

So are some young people really proud of their ASBOs? 25-year-old Ed Huck says, 'It's true. Young people will collect ASBOs as a badge of honour', although 15-year-old

Mueen Pasha disagrees: 'No, they're not collected as a badge of honour, definitely not.'

Perhaps ASBOs aren't being taken seriously because of the haphazard way they were organised in the first place. There seems to have been a serious lack of information on ASBOs given to the public which has been very detrimental. There have been reports of some people who've received ASBOs and barely knew what they were, and other reports about teenagers who had never heard of them – despite the fact that, when ASBOs were launched, David Blunkett (then Home Secretary) described them as something 'that is required to protect communities'.

One of the main concerns with ASBOs for many children's charities is the high number handed out to under-18s. It's been reported that 50% of all ASBOs have been given to children and teenagers. Another issue children's charities are worried about is the recent trend of 'naming and shaming' young people. They argue that this can destroy a child's future, making it impossible for them to turn their lives around. They also claim that ASBOs are demonising young people and stereotyping those who hang out on the streets in hooded tops or baseball caps as troublemakers. Even though they may not be committing any crimes, they are still blamed for causing problems. The Children's Society policy editor Kathy Evans justifies their behaviour: 'For many young people, hanging around on the streets with their friends is their best choice option.'

Many people have also raised concerns about the fact there aren't any ways in which to redeem yourself from an ASBO in order to shorten the time you have it. One small mistake by a police officer who thinks he has seen someone commit an ASBO-worthy crime can cost a person a minimum of two years with a cruel and unfair label. Suggestions have

been made as a way around this. 26-year-old Jennifer says, 'They should definitely be able to work ASBOs off with community service, or something like that.'

But the question remains: if ASBOs aren't working, how else do we control anti-social behaviour? 'They should either be imprisoned or fined,' says 42-year-old Roland. But should young people be spending their adolescent lives locked behind bars, especially with the running costs of a year's imprisonment at £36,000?

Instead, this money could be used to tackle anti-social behaviour before it happens and 14-year-old Paula thinks this is exactly what needs to happen. She is furious at the lack of support given to young people facing difficulties. 'The government should be helping them; we all have to help each other.'

The politicians are supposed to have our best interests at heart. But do they? Are they really interested in offering help to people who need it? I think that what's needed is a new system of counselling and support for ASBO teens – and there's no time like the present. But until this happens and while there are constant disagreements over the poor state of ASBOs, we can only imagine that the situation will continue. And with the nation split over how to deal with anti-social behaviour I wonder if it will ever be reduced and how many more young people will be harmed before it is.

About the team

This story was produced by Charlotte Lytton, 14. It was published by Reach for the Sky website.
1 January 2006

⇨ Reprinted with permission. Headliners (formerly Children's Express) is a learning through journalism programme for young people aged 8-19. www.headliners.org.
© Headliners

ASBO research published

Youth offending teams could save young people from 'badge of honour' ASBOs

Police, local authorities and sentencers must involve youth offending teams (YOTs) every time an Anti-Social Behaviour Order (ASBO) is considered for children and young people.

This urgent call was made today by the YJB as it published the first major independent study into how ASBOs are used on those under 18. Visit the YJB website to order or download the summary of the research or order a hardcopy of the full report for £8.

Researchers interviewed professionals and sentencers, young people and their parents, in 10 YOT areas to gain an insight into the effectiveness of ASBOs and to get the views and experiences of all involved. They found that:

⇨ in seven out of the 10 areas examined, YOTs had little or no involvement in the decisions that led to an ASBO being imposed
⇨ overuse of ASBOs can lead to many youngsters regarding them as a 'badge of honour'
⇨ some orders were made for five years or longer – considered by many to be a long time in a young person's life, taking them from childhood into adulthood
⇨ many young people did not understand the restrictions placed upon them, increasing the likelihood of breach
⇨ some judges and magistrates are concerned that ASBOs are being overused because they require a lower level of evidence than criminal orders.

'Let me be clear – the YJB is not against Anti-Social Behaviour Orders. They can – and do – work incredibly well,' said YJB Chairman Professor Rod Morgan. 'But for ASBOs to successfully reduce the likelihood of future anti-social behaviour, they need to be used correctly. That means exhausting every preventative measure in the community first, and ensuring that youth offending teams are not excluded from the ASBO process. Without YOT involvement, youngsters and their parents lack the support, advice and knowledge they need to ensure that they comply with their ASBOs.'

Since the research was commissioned last year, the YJB, in partnership with the Home Office and the Association of Chief Police Officers (ACPO), has issued guidance on the use of ASBOs on young people aged under the age of 18.

'The public must be protected from neighbourhood nuisance,' said Morgan. 'But for that to happen, ASBOs must be used correctly. Our guidance has already had a major impact on the way ASBOs are used but we are concerned that it is not used as widely as it should be. We are calling on the sentencers and the police to make sure that ASBOs are always used as a last resort.

'We are also calling for some fresh thinking to be injected into the youth justice debate and to look at alternatives which can lead to less crime, fewer victims and minimal use of ASBOs.'
2 November 2006

⇨ The above information is reprinted with kind permission from the Youth Justice Board. Visit www.yjb.gov.uk for more information.
© Youth Justice Board

The voice behind the hood

Young people call for an end to negative representation

A new report by YouthNet and the British Youth Council (BYC) shows the shocking extent to which young people feel they are negatively portrayed and viewed in today's society.

The unique report, debated by young people, parliamentarians and journalists in a House of Commons seminar on Tuesday 18 July 2006 gives the unaltered views of young people on subjects ranging from politicians and the media, to how they really feel about anti-social behaviour and those who engage in it.

90% of young people denounce anti-social activities and the majority accept that swearing, arguing and loud music can be anti-social

---

Mohammed (19), from YouthNet and BYC's Young People's Advisory Group, said:

'This report shows just how strongly we as young people feel about the way we are viewed in today's society. We actively consume the news in this country and yet have little voice in it, so it isn't surprising that such a large percentage of us feel we are constantly misrepresented as being anti-social.

'Negative comments from politicians and continual scare stories in the media lead to a real lack of respect for young people and greatly affect our relationships with older generations.'

Katie (17), also from the Young People's Advisory Group, said:

'Results from this research show that most young people feel as strongly about anti-social behaviour as older people and we do not want to be judged solely on the actions of a few troublemaking individuals. What we want is more of the positive things that we do to be celebrated and our views included in public debates.

'We do have a voice, and it's time for people to listen.'

Headline findings

⇨ 90% of young people denounce anti-social activities and the majority accept that swearing, arguing and loud music can be anti-social.

⇨ 98% of young people feel the media always, often or sometimes represent them as anti-social.

⇨ 75% of young people lose respect for politicians when they say negative things about young people.

⇨ Over 80% of young people believe the way they are portrayed leads to older people respecting them less.

Key recommendations

⇨ Politicians – Take more time to engage young people in discussions, by visiting schools and holding youth surgeries.

⇨ Journalists – Try to balance negative stories with more positive ones and include young people's comments in more articles.

⇨ Public sector – Create more opportunities for young people to interact with older generations.

At the seminar, young people from the Advisory Group discussed the concerns highlighted in the report and heard responses from Parliamentary Under Secretary of State for Children, Young People and Families, Parmjit Dhanda MP, and Libby Brooks, author of *The story of childhood: growing up in modern Britain* and the *Guardian* newspaper's Deputy Comment Editor.

Parliamentary Under Secretary of State for Children, Young People and Families, Parmjit Dhanda MP, said:

'I am very pleased to be here today to listen to the findings of this research. The issue of how we create more of a sense of mutual respect in communities is at the heart of the Government's Respect agenda and I welcome this opportunity to hear ideas and views from young people. It's really important to acknowledge that anti-social behaviour is not just committed by young people and I am looking forward to talking to the young people's Respect Advisory Group today about what more we could do to celebrate the positive behaviour of the majority of young people.'

The launch of this report and the seminar are the first stages in the new Respect campaign; a joint venture between YouthNet and the BYC aimed at putting young people's voices at the heart of a debate that appears to be all about them, yet currently lacks their view.
July 2006

⇨ The above information is reprinted with kind permission from TheSite.org. Visit www.thesite.org for more information.

© TheSite.org

Positive press

71% of news about young people is negative. Children's Express journalists Samantha and Samir report on why and what can be done about it

Can you think of a good reason why you would put the UK Secretary of State for Culture, Media and Sport, a bunch of adult journalists, the heads of the world's leading children's organisations, a load of middle-aged men in suits and two young reporters from Children's Express in the same room for over five hours?

> **71% of press stories about young people are negative, 33% of them are only concerned with crime and only 8% carry quotes from young people themselves**

Well, there are lots of reasons why last October we all met in Bath to discuss children's rights and press freedom. You would think that we'd all be able to agree on how to stop the negative portrayal of young people in the media but unfortunately it wasn't quite so simple. But it's not surprising as it's a really big issue.

Before we went to the conference we did quite a bit of research on the subject. We were shocked when we read the statistics – 71% of press stories about young people are negative, 33% of them are only concerned with crime and only 8% of stories about young people carry quotes from young people themselves.

With such alarming figures we were really keen to push this point at the conference and were lucky enough to get an interview with Tessa Jowell, the Secretary of State for Culture, Media and Sport. We asked her what she thought about the way young people are represented in the media:

'By and large I think the representation of children is fine and within the terms of the code that newspapers are intended to operate,'

For a moment we wondered if she ever read the papers but she went on to say:

'I sometimes think children and young people are presented too much as the source of the problem: they focus on children who get into trouble.'

Lynn Geldof, the Regional Communicators Adviser for UNICEF, also spoke about the issue and told the conference:

'The representation of children in the mass media today is a problem. We do not hear enough from the children and the young people themselves. This situation is harming them and doing society no favours.'

What about the people who actually report the news? The BBC journalist John Sweeney said the media are like white blood cells, if everything is okay then you are fine but if it's not then you are in trouble. 'We're interested when things go wrong. That's the nature of the media, we don't do good stories.'

The people we spoke to all seemed to agree with us, that the way we (young people) are stereotyped is something that needs to be changed but the big question is how?

Tessa Jowell seemed to think that it was organisations like Children's Express that could make the difference.

We agree that at Children's Express we are in a good position to do this, but unfortunately we cannot do this alone. We would like editors, particularly of the tabloid press, to change the way they report on young people in their papers.

Let's have less of the 'yobs attack teachers' and more of the 'young person wins science and technology robotics award' please!

About the team

This story was produced by Samantha, 13, and Samir, 16. It was published by G-Nation.
23 January 2006

⇨ Reprinted with permission. Headliners (formerly Children's Express) is a learning through journalism programme for young people aged 8-19. www.headliners.org.

© Headliners

So... you say you saw some scouts helping an old lady across the street?

NEWS DESK

Let's see...."Horrified bystander witnessess teenage gang force helpless granny into path of speeding motorists!"

NEWS DESK

Fear of young people

Childhood is changing, but 'paedophobia' makes things worse

Britain is in danger of becoming a nation fearful of its young people, compounding the problems of troubled childhood-adult transitions, according to new research from the Institute for Public Policy Research (ippr) to be published next month. The research shows that British adults are less likely than those in other European countries to intervene to stop teenagers committing antisocial behaviour.

ippr's research comes after an extensive debate on the 'problems of modern youth' by academics, practitioners, commentators and even the Archbishop of Canterbury. The 200-page report analyses evidence from across the world and concludes that both the frequent condemnation of teenagers and recent attempts to absolve them from blame are misplaced. The report says that changes in the family, local communities and the economy have combined to cause deep inequalities in the transition to modern adult life and leave increasing numbers of young people incapable of growing up safely and successfully.

ippr's report will say that a lack of adult supervision of teenagers in communities where adults do not know their neighbours and where teenage groups go unsupervised on the street has increased the risk of youth crime and violence. It shows that young people who claim not to spend time with their parents commit more antisocial behaviour.

The report shows that:

⇨ Last year more than 1.5 million Britons thought about moving away from their local area due to young people hanging around and 1.7 million avoided going out after dark as a direct result. Last year Britons were three times more likely to cite young people hanging around as a problem than they were to complain about noisy neighbours. In 1992 it was just 1.75 times more likely.

⇨ Britons are more likely than other Europeans to say that young people are predominantly responsible for antisocial behaviour, and they are also more likely to cite 'lack of discipline' as the root cause: 79 per cent of Britons thought this underpinned antisocial behaviour, compared to 69 per cent of Spaniards, 62 per cent of Italians and 58 per cent of French people.

But the report cites evidence that:

⇨ British adults are less likely than those in other European countries to stop teenagers committing antisocial behaviour. 65 per cent of Germans, 52 per cent of Spanish and 50 per cent of Italians would be willing to intervene if they saw a group of 14-year-old boys vandalising a bus shelter, compared to just 34 per cent of Britons. Thirty-nine per cent of Britons unwilling to get involved claimed they feared being physically attacked, 14 per cent were scared of later reprisals

and 12 per cent feared being verbally abused.

The report also shows that participation in structured youth activities is better for young people than unstructured youth clubs. ippr's analysis of data from cohorts born in 1958 and 1970 shows that by the age of 30, young people who participated in sports or community centres at age 16 were three per cent less likely to be depressed; five per cent less likely to be single, separated or divorced; three per cent less likely to be in social housing; two per cent less likely to have no qualifications; four per cent less likely not to have achieved level two qualifications; and three per cent less likely to be on a low income. Attending uniformed activities (like the Scouts, sports or martial arts) meant you were three per cent less likely not to achieve level two qualifications, three per cent less likely to be on a low income and less likely to be depressed in adulthood. Young people who attended church were two per cent less likely to smoke in adulthood, three per cent more likely to experience psychological distress in adulthood and less likely to have no qualifications, low income or be an offender.

These results stand in marked contrast to youth club attendees, who were six per cent more likely to smoke in adulthood, one per cent

more likely to be a single parent, one per cent more likely to be a victim of crime, five per cent more likely to have no qualifications and seven per cent more likely not to have reached level two qualifications. They were also five per cent more likely to be an offender and two per cent more likely to be on a low income.

Nick Pearce, ippr Director, said:

'The debate about childhood in Britain is polarised between false opposites: that either children or adults are to blame. It also ignores inequalities in the transition to adulthood. Many children are safer, healthier and better educated than in the past, whilst others suffer complex, traumatic routes through adolescence. Complex structural changes to our society, coupled with changes to how young people behave, have produced this situation.

'A rise in social paedophobia will simply make matters worse. In the past, local parents tended to look out for children in a community, deciding what behaviour was appropriate, how it should be dealt with and supporting each other in doing so. In closer-knit communities, adults supervised their neighbours' children. These days, adults tend to turn a blind eye or cross over on the other side of the road rather than intervene in the discipline of another person's child, often because they fear they might be attacked.'

Freedom's Orphans: Raising Youth in a Changing World will be published next month (Nov) and will recommend that every secondary school pupil (from 11-16 years old) should participate in at least two hours a week of structured and purposeful extracurricular activities – like martial arts, drama clubs, sports, Scouts, and so on. This would take place through extended school hours of between 8am-6pm and would involve a legal extension of the school day. Parents who did not ensure their child attended two hours a week of activities could be fined, in the same way as parents are punished for their child's persistent truancy.

The report argues that this will help promote educational attainment, develop personal skills and reduce problem behaviour across adolescence and into young adulthood. It would also provide the opportunity to mix with non-deviant peers, to be mentored by adult activity leaders, and work towards clear goals like badges and belts.

ippr research shows that at the moment, just one in four young people have access to 'structured' youth activities. There are 11,095 youth clubs in England providing for 1.2million 11- to 16-year-olds. There are 4.6million 11- to 16-year-olds in England to be provided for.

Notes

Respondents were asked how confident they would feel intervening personally if they saw a small group of 14-year-old boys vandalising a bus shelter:

⇨ in Great Britain, 30 per cent would definitely not challenge them, 32 per cent would probably not challenge them, 23 per cent would probably challenge them and 11 per cent would challenge them;

⇨ in Germany, seven per cent would definitely not challenge them, 21 per cent would probably not challenge them, 40 per cent would probably challenge them and 24 per cent would challenge them;

⇨ in Italy, 13 per cent would definitely not challenge them, 28 per cent would probably not challenge them, 37 per cent would probably challenge them and 30 per cent would challenge them;

⇨ in Spain, 9 per cent didn't know, 17 per cent would definitely not challenge them, 24 per cent would probably not challenge them, 34 per cent would probably challenge them and 17 per cent would challenge them. Percentages may not total to 100 due to rounding;

⇨ in France, 19 per cent would definitely not challenge them, 34 per cent would probably not challenge them, 31 per cent would probably challenge them and 9 per cent would challenge them;

⇨ in the Netherlands, 19 per cent would definitely not challenge them, 30 per cent would probably not challenge them, 30 per cent would probably challenge them and 13 per cent would challenge them.

Britons were asked how likely would you be to intervene if you saw two or three teenagers...?

⇨ Spray painting on a building in your street – 36 per cent definitely ask them to stop; 24 per cent probably ask them to stop; 21 per cent probably don't ask them to stop; 18 per cent definitely don't ask them to stop.

⇨ Damaging property or cars in your street – 44 per cent definitely ask them to stop; 24 per cent probably ask them to stop; 15 per cent probably don't ask them to stop; 15 per cent definitely don't ask them to stop.

⇨ Being loud, rowdy or noisy outside your home – 36 per cent definitely ask them to stop; 27 per cent probably ask them to stop; 21 per cent probably don't ask them to stop; 14 per cent definitely don't ask them to stop.

⇨ Abusing, harassing or insulting an elderly person in the street – 68 per cent would definitely ask them to stop; 22 per cent probably ask them to stop; four per cent probably don't ask them to stop; five per cent definitely don't ask them to stop.

22 October 2006

⇨ The above information is re-printed with kind permission from the Institute for Public Policy Research. Visit www.ippr.org.uk for more information.

© ippr

Help! I'm a victim

TheSite finds you the right kind of help, quickly

What should you do if you are a victim of crime?

Report the crime to the police. In many cases the police will come to the scene of the crime, but if the crime is not serious and the offender has left the scene, officers may take details from you over the telephone instead.

The officers taking the details will give you a crime reference number and tell you how to find out about the progress of your case. They will also tell you if someone is arrested and charged in connection with your case. If you move house or have any updates or further details on your case, keep the police informed.

If you have been a victim of:
⇨ Rape: visit the Rape Crisis Federation.
⇨ Domestic violence: visit Women's Aid.

The Victim's Charter

If you have been a victim of crime the 1996 Victim's Charter sets out the standards of service that you or your family can expect from the criminal justice agencies. It also explains how you can complain if the standards are not met.

You can expect:
⇨ A crime you have reported to be investigated and to receive information about what happens.
⇨ The chance to explain how the crime has affected you, and your interests to be taken into account.
⇨ If you have to go to court as a witness, to be treated with respect and sensitivity.
⇨ To be offered emotional and practical support.

Where can I get support?

Victim Support: The police will ask for your consent to pass your

TheSite.org

details on to Victim Support. Victim Support is an independent charity which helps people cope with the effects of crime. They provide free and confidential support and information to help you deal with your experience, including:
⇨ Someone to talk to;
⇨ Information on police and court procedure;
⇨ Liaison with other organisations on your behalf;
⇨ Information on compensation and insurance matters;
⇨ Contact with other sources of help.

Victim Support can also arrange for a volunteer to accompany you to the police station and to court.

VOICE UK: This organisation helps people with learning disabilities who have been a victim of crime or abuse.

Release of prisoners

If you have been the victim of a sexual or violent offence and the offender has been sentenced to more than one year in prison, the *Release*

of Prisoners leaflet explains the role of the National Probation Service in telling you or your family about what has happened to an offender after he or she has been sentenced.

You can ring the Victim Helpline to find out the due date for the prisoner's release, or if you have received unwanted contact from a prisoner call: 0845 7585 112.

Criminal Injuries compensation

If you have been assaulted or your property has been stolen or damaged you may be entitled to claim compensation from Criminal Injuries. If you think you may qualify take a note of:
⇨ Any expenses you have had as a result of the offence, for example, medical charges or the cost of repairing or replacing your property;
⇨ Any loss of earnings you may have suffered;
⇨ Any income you may have received as a result of the offence, for example DSS benefit.

⇨ The above information is re-printed with kind permission from TheSite.org. Visit www.thesite.org for more information.

© *TheSite.org*

How crime can affect you

Information from Victim Support

Crime can affect people in many different ways. Many people are surprised how emotional they feel after being a victim of crime. These strong emotions can make you feel even more unsettled and confused. People around you such as friends, partners and children will also be affected. They may feel similar emotions to yours, as well as concern for you. But many people find that others around them expect them to 'get over it'. This is not always helpful if what you really want to do is talk about how you feel.

How you react to a crime will also depend on:
⇨ the type of crime
⇨ whether you know the person who committed the crime
⇨ the support you get from your family, friends, the police and other people you come into contact with
⇨ things that have happened to you

in the past – such as other hurtful events.

The effects can last for a long time. Even if other people do not think of the crime as very serious, you may still find you have a severe reaction. For example, a burglary can affect someone's life just as badly as an assault, even though nobody may have been physically hurt during the burglary.

Most victims of crime do not suffer any long-term harm. But some people do develop long-term problems, such as depression or anxiety-related illnesses. And a few experience a severe, long-lasting reaction after a crime known as post-traumatic stress disorder. This is a medical term used to describe a pattern of symptoms found in a person who has experienced a traumatic event. However you've been affected, we can provide information and support to help you cope with your feelings.

One of the things that can make crime hard to cope with is knowing that it was committed deliberately. Unlike an accident or illness, where there is normally no harm intended, people who commit a crime have done it with intention to cause harm. If you are the victim, this can make you feel very powerless and vulnerable. This can be especially difficult to deal with if the crime is repeated or ongoing which is often the case with domestic violence or racial harassment.

It is not unusual to have strong reactions after being a victim of crime. You may find it helps to talk to us or you can find out more about how we can help with some specific crimes.

⇨ The above information is reprinted with kind permission from Victim Support. Visit www.victimsupport.org.uk for more information.

© Victim Support

'Smarter justice'

'Smarter justice' plans aim to rebalance system in favour of victim

The criminal justice bill, the 60th Home Office bill since Tony Blair came to power, implements the prime minister's pledge to 'rebalance the criminal justice system in favour of the victim'

**By Alan Travis,
Home Affairs Editor**

and create a system of 'smarter justice'. It is expected to be introduced in April or May next year and will be accompanied by three other anti-crime bills with new powers to tackle organised crime, open up the probation service to competition and scrap the use of juries in serious fraud trials.

The Home Office said the new criminal justice bill will include the shake-up in sentencing outlined last week and the new 'instant justice' powers to tackle antisocial behaviour, including evicting rowdy neighbours, proposed yesterday.

A battery of new powers are to be included, among them violent offender orders that will impose restrictions on violent criminals after their sentence ends, such as where they can live and who they can associate with.

It will also create a new offence to deal with violent pornography, cut compensation for those who have suffered a miscarriage of justice and introduce a generic community sentence for young offenders.

Changes to the sentencing powers of the courts will include restoring discretion to judges over sentence reductions for early guilty pleas and requiring unanimous parole decisions before life-sentence prisoners can be released.

The organised crime bill will break new ground by introducing a 'super-asbo' – a serious crime prevention order – which will be used to disrupt the activities of major gangsters in the run-up to their trials, or minor players by freezing their assets and other measures.

The fraud (trials without jury) bill, which is to be the first Home Office bill to be published, will scrap the use of juries in serious fraud cases on the approval of the lord chief justice. In the past four years there were 26 fraud trials that lasted more than six months.

The final piece of Home Office legislation, the offender management bill, will abolish local probation boards and allow regional offender managers to commission probation services from the voluntary and private sectors as well as the probation service. It will also strengthen the law against smuggling banned articles into prison.

Nick Clegg, the Liberal Democrats' home affairs spokesman, said there had already been 59 Home Office bills creating more than 3,000 new offences since 1997, yet reoffending rates had risen and fear of crime remained alarmingly high.

'More than 50 sections of the 2003 Criminal Justice Act haven't been put into effect, and yet John Reid has proposed new legislation to replace it altogether. This is panic, push-button government at its worst.'

Juliet Lyon of the Prison Reform Trust added that prison numbers had risen from 60,000 in 1997 to almost 80,000 today. Despite Mr Blair promising social inclusion and public safety in 1997, he had ended up seeking solutions in prison and punishment instead of health, education and communities.

But Roger Howard of Crime Concern, the national crime prevention organisation, welcomed the measures: 'We've long believed that the answer to the criminal justice system is to become smarter, rather than tougher. Today's criminal justice bill promises to put the victim at the heart of the criminal justice system. Anything that helps the offender to understand better the effects of their actions must be welcomed.'

He said the probation legislation also made sense as it would contract out the work to the best service provider, after years of suffering a 60% reoffending rate.

The legislation was also welcomed by Paul Cavadino of Nacro, the crime reduction charity, who said the involvement of charities in rehabilitating offenders would improve law and order much more than toughening sentences or fining the parents of badly behaved children.

16 November 2006

Main points

⇨ Criminal justice bill to introduce sentencing shake-up and more police powers to tackle anti-social behaviour. It will cap compensation for wrongful conviction; make parole board decisions unanimous; and create new offence of violent pornography.

⇨ Organised crime bill will introduce serious crime prevention orders and create new offences of encouraging or assisting a criminal act.

⇨ Offender management bill to bring voluntary organisations and private companies into probation and replace probation boards with trusts.

⇨ Bill to scrap juries in serious fraud trials on the approval of the lord chief justice.

Reporting a crime

Information from the Home Office

If you've been the victim of a crime it's really important to report it. We know that sometimes it's not easy to decide to come forward. But we also know that if no one reports a crime, it's as if it never happened.

If no one reports a crime, the criminal is free to commit more crime, damaging more communities and individuals.

It's also important to report crime for your own practical purposes, like getting a crime number from the police so that you can make an insurance claim.

How do I report a crime?

There are lots of ways to report a crime, including:

⇨ going to your local police station
⇨ reporting a crime anonymously
⇨ reporting non-emergency crime online.

Going to your local police station

At the police station you will be asked to provide details of the crime and make a statement about the facts of the case.

You'll receive a crime reference number that you can quote to find out about the progress of your case and to use if you're making any kind of insurance claim, for example, for a stolen mobile phone.

To find contact details for your local police station:

⇨ look in the front section of the Phone Book, under 'In an emergency', or in the Yellow Pages under 'Police'

If no one reports a crime, the criminal is free to commit more crime, damaging more communities and individuals

---

⇨ visit the Police Force finder on the UK Police Service website: www.police.uk/forces/default.asp

Reporting a crime anonymously

Crimestoppers is a completely independent organisation which allows you to provide the details of a crime, without revealing your identity.

You will not be compelled to give your name, sign any kind of statement or appear in court – all you have to do is provide the information about the crime.

For more information visit the Crimestoppers website: www.crimestoppers-uk.org

Reporting non-emergency crimes online

You can report non-emergency crimes online, saving you the trouble of having to go to your local police station.

To report a crime online visit the Non-emergency Notification website: www.online.police.uk

Can I do anything else to help the case?

Make a victim personal statement
You can also make a 'victim personal statement'. A victim personal statement allows you to explain more about the impact of the crime on you personally. The personal statement can be used by the judge or magistrate to help them decide on an appropriate sentence for the offender.

Deciding to provide a victim personal statement is completely voluntary and you can decide to make one at any point in the case.

Crimestoppers is a completely independent organisation which allows you to provide the details of a crime, without revealing your identity

To find out more read the guide Making a Victim Personal Statement and visit the Victims area of the Criminal Justice System website.

What happens next?

Once you've reported a crime you will be kept informed of developments and – depending on the outcome of the resulting investigation – you may need to appear in court as a witness.

Helping victims and witnesses come forward

To help people come forward, and take back the power from the criminals, we're improving the justice system, so that it supports and protects those who report crime.

⇨ The above information is reprinted with kind permission from the Home Office. Visit www.homeoffice.gov.uk for more information.

© Crown copyright

Some reasons people don't report crime

Information from Victims of Crime in Scotland

These are some of the reasons for not reporting crimes.

It's too trivial

It may be a minor crime, but it can still be very upsetting. The police understand this and will take the incident you report seriously.

I'm too embarrassed

Sometimes people feel embarrassed about reporting sexual crimes. The police will treat you sensitively and will not judge you. Whatever your gender, sexual orientation, race or physical ability, being a victim of a crime is traumatic.

The police won't care

If the police are very busy, they may not be able to get to you as soon as they would like. However, their job is to protect and reassure and they do care about doing that. They may not always catch the people responsible but they always try.

I don't care about what's happened

If you are not concerned or upset by what's happened, that's fine. Some people can take these things in their stride, and continue as if nothing has happened, even if it's been a serious crime. However, if you don't report it, the police won't have a chance to catch the person responsible, and they might do it again. The next time, they might pick on a person who is not so resilient as you.

I'm worried about what will happen

People worry about going to the police and perhaps having to go to court and give evidence. However, there are many organisations that can support you through the various stages. The Victims of Crime in Scotland website gives contact details. It is important for you to talk about what has happened to you and to get any reassurance and help you need.

⇨ The above information is reprinted with kind permission from Victims of Crime in Scotland. Please visit the Victims of Crime in Scotland website at www.scottishvictimsofcrime.co.uk for more information.

© Victims of Crime in Scotland

The police

Information from the Centre for Crime and Justice Studies

For most of us, the police are the visible face of the criminal justice system. The police patrol our streets, arrest the suspects, collect the evidence, and without them there would be no criminal justice system. But how much do we know about the police force and the issues and challenges it is currently facing?

Ten police basics

1 There are eight police forces in Scotland, 43 in England and Wales, and the single Police Service of Northern Ireland divided into 30 District Command Units.

> **The single biggest issue facing the police continues to be accusations and evidence of discrimination**

2 At the last review of policing in England and Wales in March 2004, there were 139,200 full-time police officers – a record number exceeding the previous year's record of 133,366 and the government target of 132,500.
3 This represents an increase of 5.4%, the largest single year increase in the last 35 years.
4 The police officers are backed up by 73,822 full-time support staff.
5 This number includes over 4,000 Community Support Officers.
6 Each police force is run by a local Police Authority and funded by local council tax and government grants.
7 Most Police Authorities are made up of nine councillors, three magistrates and five independent members and are responsible for hiring and firing the chief constable.

8 Each police force is divided into areas or divisions based at local police stations known as Basic Command Units (BCUs).
9 Each police force has part-time volunteer officers known as Special Constables.
10 London's Metropolitan Police Service is the largest police force. It employs over 31,000 officers and 12,000 support staff and covers an area of 620 square miles and a population of over 7.2 million.

Who are the police?

Police Officers are divided into ranks. The majority of the police force is made up of Police Constables (PCs). Next up Sergeant, then Inspector, Chief Inspector, Superintendent, Chief Superintendent, Assistant Chief Constable, Deputy Chief Constable, and most senior is Chief Constable. In the Metropolitan Police the senior ranks are slightly different.

On completing training, a PC in the Metropolitan Police is paid £28,383, a Sergeant is paid £36,405, and an Inspector is paid £41,586. In other forces a PC is paid £22,107 after completing training, a Sergeant is paid £31,092, and an Inspector makes £39,840.

In England and Wales there are 4,629 black or minority ethnic officers, only 3.3% of the total but an increase on last year's figures. 5.7% of support staff are black or minority ethnic. One in five police officers is now a woman, although most occupy junior ranks. Only 8.9% of officers of the rank of superintendent or above are women.

Discrimination?

The single biggest issue facing the police continues to be accusations and evidence of discrimination.

⇨ In 1999, the McPherson Inquiry found the Metropolitan Police to be 'institutionally racist' after its handling of the investigation into the murder of black teenager Stephen Lawrence.
⇨ Two years later, senior Iranian-born Met officer Ali Dizaei, who was outspoken on issues of race, was suspended amid allegations of drug dealing and involvement with prostitutes. This followed a four-year covert operation costing between £3.5 million and £7 million. Eventually he was cleared of any wrongdoing, awarded £80,000 compensation and reinstated. The Black Police Association claimed the investigation was racially motivated.

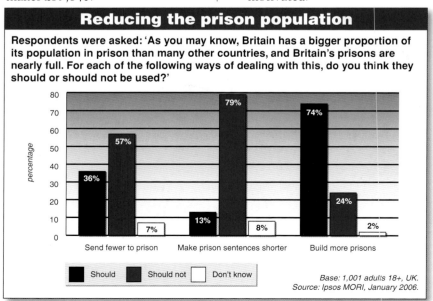

Reducing the prison population

Respondents were asked: 'As you may know, Britain has a bigger proportion of its population in prison than many other countries, and Britain's prisons are nearly full. For each of the following ways of dealing with this, do you think they should or should not be used?'

Send fewer to prison: Should 36%, Should not 57%, Don't know 7%
Make prison sentences shorter: Should 13%, Should not 79%, Don't know 8%
Build more prisons: Should 74%, Should not 24%, Don't know 2%

Should ■   Should not ■   Don't know □

Base: 1,001 adults 18+, UK.
Source: Ipsos MORI, January 2006.

- Then in 2003 an undercover BBC journalist filmed recruits at the Police National Training Centre in Warrington making racist remarks and imitating members of the Ku Klux Klan.
- In April 2004 a Met PC was suspended after making racist remarks to another recruit.
- In June 2004 the Commission for Racial Equality announced its intention to commence legal action against 14 police forces and 8 police authorities whose race equality schemes failed to meet minimum legal requirements.

80% of people in a survey performed by the Audit Commission said they were not satisfied with the levels of police patrol in their area

---

- In December 2004 an inquiry was launched after a senior Greater Manchester Police Officer made derogatory remarks about Muslims celebrating the Eid Festival. The Police Superintendents' Association supported the officer.
- The police have failed to meet targets set by the government for the recruitment of black and minority ethnic officers.

The police are attempting to reform.
- The Met have delivered 'diversity training' to 40,000 staff.

- The 'Gender Agenda' was set up to actively recruit women officers.
- Police forces now monitor officer's sexuality and the Gay Police Association reports better attitudes to gay officers and gay citizens.

Police Community Support Officers

The government has recently introduced a new kind of police officer, a Community Support Officer (CSO), intended to be highly visible, on the beat, with the aim of deterring anti-social behaviour and minor acts of criminality.

There are currently over 4,000 CSOs and the government aims to extend the numbers of CSOs and Wardens to 25,000. Starting in January 2005, the powers of CSOs have been extended to stopping and searching suspects and detaining them for up to half an hour to allow for the arrival of the police.

Critics, including some police officers, claim that the government is introducing less trained and less well-paid police by the back door and this might put the safety of the public and the CSOs in jeopardy.

Did you know?

- 80% of people in a survey performed by the Audit Commission said they were not satisfied with the levels of police patrol in their area.
- 80% of police officers surveyed by the Police Federation of England and Wales stated that they did not wish officers to be routinely armed on duty.

- A recent report published by the Institute of Public Policy Research stated that the outdated design of police stations alienates the public and hampers police effectiveness. The report recommended the return of police boxes in the style of Japanese Kobans.

Useful links

- http://www.police.uk A site providing links to official police forces in the United Kingdom and related organisations.
- http://www.acpo.police.uk The Association of Chief Police Officers develops policing policy in England and Wales.
- http://www.met.police.uk The homepage of the Metropolitan Police Service.
- http://www.bawp.org The British Association of Women in Policing represents the interests of women officers throughout the United Kingdom.
- http://www.nationalbpa.com The homepage of the National Black Police Association representing the interests of black and minority ethnic police service employees.
- http://www.gay.police.uk The homepage of the Gay Police Association representing the interests of gay and lesbian police service employees.

- The above information is reprinted with kind permission from the Centre for Crime and Justice Studies. Visit www.crimeinfo.org.uk for more information.

© CCJS

Police want new powers of 'instant justice'

Town centre bans and car crushing orders – without going to court

By Alan Travis,
Home Affairs Editor

Police are pressing ministers for radical new powers to dispense instant justice, including the immediate exclusion of 'yobs' from town centres at night, and bans on street gang members associating with each other, the *Guardian* has learned.

Senior officers say the powers would be the 'modern equivalent of a clip round the ear from the local bobby' and would ensure the introduction of neighbourhood policing across England and Wales has 'bite' and meets public expectations.

Ministers are considering extending police summary powers as a crucial part of Tony Blair's drive to 'rebalance' the criminal justice system.

The powers have been proposed by Surrey's Assistant Chief Constable, Mark Rowley, the Association of Chief Police Officers' spokesman on modernising the way police work. They include:

⇨ Powers for police officers to tackle 'town centre yobs' by immediately excluding an offender from the town centre at night 'for an appropriate period' when they are issued with an informal warning or a fixed-penalty fine.

⇨ Powers to tackle disorder by giving the neighbourhood constable, who understands the local context, the right to issue a three-month ban on gangs who cause repeat disorder on estates from associating with each other in public or frequenting a particular location. The ban could include a requirement to clear up local damage. Breaching the order would lead to an immediate court appearance with a possible fine, parenting order or ASBO.

⇨ Powers to tackle 'the yob driver': those repeatedly stopped in an unregistered car with no insurance, no driving licence or MOT, could face immediate seizure of the car which would be crushed. An instant interim driving ban would be imposed pending a court appearance.

⇨ Tackling knife crime by enabling 'reasonable suspicion' for stop and search to be based on previous convictions.

Mr Rowley told Acpo's *Police Professional* magazine that the service had seen such an erosion in its formal and informal powers that it was now at risk of being no more than an agency of referral to a 'slow and inaccessible' criminal justice system.

The proposals he cited could prove the modern equivalent of the 'mythical clip around the ear from the local bobby' that the media and the public said they wanted. Such summary justice proposals would make powers, already theoretically available through the courts, available for instant delivery on the streets with an appeal to the court later.

He said that the massive investment in dedicated neighbourhood policing teams was increasing expectations among local people for immediate effective action to tackle anti-social behaviour.

'It therefore is time to debate whether constables should be given substantial additional, discretionary, summary powers to meet these challenges ... Such powers would effectively bring existing criminal justice system powers to the street.

'We could move from the police referring and the courts sentencing to the police solving and the courts providing scrutiny,' said Mr Rowley, adding that they would provide neighbourhood policing with the 'bite' the public expects.

But the proposals have alarmed human rights campaigners. Shami Chakrabarti of Liberty said: 'This looks like instant police justice and a return to the infamous sus laws. Surely the many officers who are proud of our consent-based policing tradition will resent the idea of being legislator, judge and jury on the cheap?'

Alan Gordon, vice-chairman of the Police Federation, which represents rank-and-file officers, said he was not sure that he was in favour of the police imposing any form of sentence: 'The enforcement of the law and then a form of punishment should be two separate processes.'

An Acpo spokeswoman last night confirmed that the proposals put forward by Mr Rowley and the workforce modernisation committee were being explored. A more detailed set of proposals would be worked up before being formally proposed to ministers.

15 August 2006

Tackling anti-social behaviour

Information from the National Audit Office

The majority of people who received an anti-social behaviour intervention, in a sample of cases examined by the National Audit Office, did not re-engage in anti-social behaviour. But, for a number of perpetrators, interventions had limited impact. 17 per cent of the population perceive high levels of anti-social behaviour in their area and the cost to government agencies of responding to reports of anti-social behaviour in England and Wales is approximately £3.4 billion per year.

A report published today by the National Audit Office found that around 65 per cent in a sample of 893 people who received some form of anti-social behaviour intervention did not engage in further anti-social behaviour. There was, however, a hard core of perpetrators for whom interventions had limited impact. 20 per cent of the people in the sample received 55 per cent of all interventions issued.

The study looked at the impact of three of the most commonly used interventions: warning letters, Acceptable Behaviour Contracts and Anti-Social Behaviour Orders. The success rate for those receiving warning letters or Acceptable Behaviour Contracts were similar, with around two-thirds receiving just one form of intervention from the authorities. However, over half of those who received the strongest form of intervention – an Anti-Social Behaviour Order (ASBO) – breached the Order, and one-third did so on five or more occasions. Forty per cent of people who received an Anti-Social Behaviour Order had received an earlier anti-social behaviour intervention and 80 per cent had previous criminal convictions.

The Home Office's Anti-Social Behaviour Unit has successfully supported local areas to tackle anti-social behaviour through funding 373 Anti-Social Behaviour Co-ordinators, promoting the use of new tools and powers and providing training to practitioners. Whilst 21 per cent of the population perceived high levels of anti-social behaviour in 2002-03, by 2005-06 this had fallen to 17 per cent. There is, however, a significant regional disparity in levels of perception, from 29 per cent of people in London perceiving high levels of anti-social behaviour to seven per cent in Essex and Lincolnshire. In general the young and least well off are disproportionately adversely affected.

In four of the 12 areas visited by the NAO, local co-ordinators working to tackle anti-social behaviour were concerned that a lack of capacity and experience of using anti-social behaviour legislation within their local authorities' legal services departments meant that breaches were not always dealt with in a timely manner, creating frustration in the local community. This frustration appears to be compounded by fear of reprisal for individuals who report incidents, and concerns that witness intimidation is a factor in the breakdown of legal processes when dealing with breaches of intervention.

Local agencies would be better placed to target their interventions more effectively if the Home Office undertook formal evaluation of the success of different interventions and the impact of providing support services in conjunction with enforcement. International research suggests that preventive programmes, such as education, counselling and training, can be a cost-effective way of addressing anti-social behaviour. The Home Office, together with other Departments, is taking this forward through the Respect Action Plan and the Government is also currently considering further legislation to address anti-social behaviour.

Sir John Bourn said today:

'Whilst 65 per cent of people in our case review did not go on to commit any further anti-social behaviour after receiving one anti-social behaviour intervention, there is a hard core of individuals who repeatedly behave in an anti-social way and for whom more action is needed.

'The Home Office should formally evaluate the success of different interventions and the impact of combining enforcement interventions with support services to better advise Anti-Social Behaviour Co-ordinators at a local level. They should also consider developing and implementing further more preventive measures to tackle the causes of anti-social behaviour.'

7 December 2006

⇨ The above information is reprinted with kind permission from the National Audit Office. Visit www.nao.org.uk for more information.

© National Audit Office

Going to court

Information from the National Youth Agency

On average a person accused of an offence will go to court about four times. The process can be quite slow – on average about two or three months from the time you first go to court and the final outcome. Obviously in some cases it will be a lot quicker e.g. if your case gets 'thrown out' because there is not enough evidence or if your case is simple to deal with.

Where will you be during the time from the first court hearing to the final outcome? In most cases you are allowed to be at home (perhaps with conditions like staying at home at night). In some cases you may be required to stay in another place – perhaps even a prison.

Getting legal advice for court

If you are going to any kind of court it is important to get legal advice before going in. You may have already had contact with a solicitor at the police station. Otherwise you can contact one that you find in yellow pages or wait until you get to the court where there will be a 'duty solicitor' available for quick advice. In some cases the duty solicitor will go into court with you there and then, otherwise (s)he will be able to help you get another solicitor.

Does it cost to have a solicitor?

If the duty solicitor is going in with you it is free. It can also be free if you are 17 or under or 18 and over and meet the low income criteria for legal aid. However, in the end it is up to the court to decide if you get legal aid. The main situation where you would be less likely to get it is where the case is a simple one that you are capable of representing yourself in. To find out more have a free introductory talk with a solicitor (under the Green Card system).

Where will my case be heard?

If you are 17 or less your case will normally be heard in a court specially designed for young people called the Youth Court. If you are 18 or over you will usually go to the magistrates' court initially and then continue in this court or go to the Crown Court (e.g. if your case is more serious). There are more details below.

Magistrates' court

A magistrate (sometimes known as a Justice of the Peace or JP) is usually an unpaid member of the public with special training to hear criminal cases. Usually three magistrates sit to hear a case and they are given special legal advice by a clerk. In some cases a legally qualified magistrate known as a stipendiary magistrate can hear cases and sits alone. A magistrates' court hears cases of criminal law, family law, licensing law as well as other types of less common cases.

Youth courts

Youth courts are part of the magistrates' court. They deal with young people 17 and under. If you are under 16 you must be accompanied by a parent or guardian or social worker. Youth courts take place in front of at least two magistrates who have extra understanding of youth justice issues. The other side (known as the prosecution) will have a lawyer putting their case. You have a right to a lawyer – this is normally free under the legal aid system. A youth court is not just about punishment – its job is also to protect your welfare.

Crown Court

If a criminal case is very serious the magistrates will send it to be heard in the Crown Court. If you are under 18 and you have committed a serious offence you will still normally be tried in the youth court although if the magistrates think it is too serious they will send the case to the Crown Court. The Crown Court is the only court which uses a jury to decide whether you are guilty or not. The family proceedings court is another part of the magistrates' court.

County courts

County courts hear cases of civil law. They are usually heard by a judge without a jury. A judge is a qualified lawyer with lots of legal experience. Some county courts are also divorce courts and family courts. They hear private cases and can issue protection and care orders.

If a case is very complicated or involves very large sums of money then it will be heard in the High Court. The High Court also has certain extra powers to look at the way public organisations like local authorities carry out their duties. This is known as judicial review.

⇨ The above information is reprinted with kind permission from the National Youth Agency. Visit www.youthinformation.com for more information.

Why the prison system needs reform

Information from the Howard League for Penal Reform

The prison population is at an all-time high

⇨ The UK is the most punitive nation in Western Europe.

⇨ In 2003, England and Wales imprisoned 141 people per 100,000 population.

⇨ The prison population hit an all time high on 1 December 2006 when it reached 80,175.

⇨ In the ten years to 2003, the prison population increased by 66%, in the case of women, 191%.

⇨ The rapid growth in the prison population has not been fuelled by escalating crime rates nor by an increase in the number of offenders appearing before the courts. Rather, harsher sentencing has resulted in our ever-escalating prison population.

Prison is not being used as a last resort

⇨ Home Office data reveal that about 78% of people sentenced to immediate custody in 2003 had committed non-violent offences (i.e. offences that did not involve violence, sex or robbery).

⇨ 15% of people remanded to prison in 2003 were subsequently given a non-custodial sentence.

Prison is expensive

⇨ During 2003-2004, it cost an average of £27,320 per year to keep someone in prison.

⇨ To build a new prison costs the equivalent of two district hospitals or 60 primary schools.

Prison is not working

⇨ 61% of all prisoners released in 2001 were reconvicted within two years

⇨ 73% of young male offenders. released 2001 were reconvicted within two years.

Prison is a brutalising and damaging experience

⇨ During 2004, 95 people killed themselves in prison service care. This included 50 people on remand and 13 women.

⇨ In addition, a 14-year-old boy took his own life in a Secure Training Centre in 2004.

⇨ Data show that in 2003, 30% of women, 65% of females under 21 and 6% of men in prison harmed themselves.

⇨ The above information is re-printed with kind permission from the Howard League for Penal Reform. Visit www.howardleague.org for more.
© Howard League for Penal Reform

The basic rights of prisoners

Information from Liberty

Reception

On reception into prison, you will be searched and may be photographed. The prison authorities will keep any property that you are not allowed to have with you in prison. A list will be made on arrival of all property and you must be given the opportunity to check it is correct before signing it. All cash must be paid into an account, which is under the governor's control. All prisoners should be issued on arrival with a copy of the Prisoners' Information Handbook. A copy of the Prison Rules must be made available to any prisoner who requests it.

Prisoners' rights

Prisoners retain certain basic rights, which survive despite imprisonment. The rights of access to the courts and of respect for one's bodily integrity – that is, not to be assaulted – are such fundamental rights. Others may be recognised as the law develops. Prisoners lose only those civil rights that are taken away either expressly by an Act of Parliament or by necessary implication. For example, one right taken away by statute is that prisoners detained following conviction do not have a right to vote. The test in every case is whether the right is fundamental and whether there is anything in the Prison Act 1952, the Prison Rules 1999 or elsewhere which authorises the prison authorities to limit such a right.

One right taken away by statute is that prisoners detained following conviction do not have a right to vote

---

The test now applied is that the State can only place limits on prisoners' rights if they are necessary for the prevention of crime or for prison security. Any limitations placed upon such rights must also be proportionate to the aim that the authorities are seeking to achieve. There are a large number of cases that have been heard by the European Court of Human Rights (ECHR) which help clarify the extent to which limitations can be imposed.

Prisoners retain certain basic rights, which survive despite imprisonment. The rights of access to the courts and of respect for one's bodily integrity are such fundamental rights

Prison Rules

In law, the Prison Rules have legal force only in so far as the Prison Act 1952 gives authority for the Rule: legal challenges to the Rules have been successful in cases where the courts have held that the Prison Act 1952 does not authorise the scope of a particular Rule. The Prison Rules provide a structure and framework for the regulation of prison life. Breach of the Rules by the prison authorities does not of itself give you the right to sue in the courts for damages.

More detailed instructions are given in the Standing Orders and Prison Service Orders and Instructions. These are internal directives, which govern the conduct of prison life issued to prison governors and prison officers. They do not have any direct legal force in that they can be challenged if they breach the scope of the Prison Act or Prison Rules. They are, however, a vital source of information about prisoners' rights and entitlements and can provide important evidence as to the proper practice that should be adopted by the prison authorities. A failure to follow the guidance contained in these documents cannot amount to a denial of a prisoner's legitimate expectation.

⇨ The above information is reprinted with kind permission from Liberty. Visit www.yourrights.org.uk for more information.

© Liberty

World prison population – key points

Information from the International Centre for Prison Studies

⇨ More than 9.25 million people are held in penal institutions throughout the world, mostly as pre-trial detainees (remand prisoners) or as sentenced prisoners. Almost half of these are in the United States (2.19m), China (1.55m plus pre-trial detainees and prisoners in 'administrative detention') or Russia (0.87m).

⇨ The United States has the highest prison population rate in the world, some 738 per 100,000 of the national population, followed by Russia (611), St Kitts & Nevis (547), US Virgin Is. (521), Turkmenistan (c.489), Belize (487), Cuba (c.487), Palau (478), British Virgin Is. (464), Bermuda (463), Bahamas (462), Cayman Is. (453), American Samoa (446), Belarus (426) and Dominica (419).

⇨ However, more than three-fifths of countries (61%) have rates below 150 per 100,000. (The rate in England and Wales – 148 per 100,000 of the national population – is above the mid-point in the World List.)

⇨ Prison population rates vary considerably between different regions of the world, and between different parts of the same continent. For example:
↳ in Africa the median rate for western African countries is 37 whereas for southern African countries it is 267;
↳ in the Americas the median rate for south American countries is 165.5 whereas for Caribbean countries it is 324;
↳ in Asia the median rate for south central Asian countries (mainly the Indian sub-continent) is 57 whereas for (ex-Soviet) central Asian countries it is 292;
↳ in Europe the median rate for southern European countries is 90 whereas for central and eastern European countries it is 185;
↳ in Oceania (including Australia and New Zealand) the median rate is 124.5.

⇨ Prison populations are growing in many parts of the world. Updated information on countries included in previous editions of the World Prison Population List shows that prison populations have risen in 73% of these countries (in 64% of countries in Africa, 84% in the Americas, 81% in Asia, 66% in Europe and 75% in Oceania).

October 2006

⇨ The above information is reprinted with kind permission from the International Centre for Prison Studies. Visit www.prisonstudies.org for more information.

© ICPS

About women's imprisonment

Information from Women in Prison

The women's prison population stands at nearly 4,500. It increased by 173% over the ten years to 2004 even though the nature and seriousness of women's offending has not been getting worse. The men's prison population rose by 50% over the same period. It is the case that 'these women are rarely serious, violent offenders and they generally pose little risk to public safety.' [1] And 'the evidence suggests that the courts are imposing more severe sentences on women for less serious offences.' [2]

The pattern of women's offending is very different to men and poses a lower level of risk to the public

Women prisoners are a different constituency to male prisoners for several reasons:

⇨ The pattern of women's offending is very different to men and poses a lower level of risk to the public.

⇨ Women prisoners are much more likely to be solely responsible for the care of children

women in prison

and the maintenance of a home than male prisoners. Because of this, prison impacts disproportionately harshly on many women prisoners, often resulting in the loss of a home and serious disruption to the lives of their children.

⇨ The huge difference in size between the male and female prison populations means the specific needs of women prisoners have been overlooked (there are more than 70,000 men in prison). The small number of women's prisons creates logistical problems, and women prisoners are likely to be held further from home than men.

⇨ Women prisoners suffer a more severe range of social exclusion problems than men, particularly high levels of abuse and domestic violence and mental health

problems. Prison is known to have more serious psychological implications for women (there were 27 self-inflicted deaths in women's prisons in 2003/4). Self-injury is very common throughout women's prisons.

Footnotes

[1] Fawcett Society, *Women and the Criminal Justice System* (2004)
[2] Home Office, *Women's Offending Reduction Programme Action Plan* (2004)

⇨ The above information is reprinted with kind permission from Women in Prison. Visit www.womeninprison.org.uk for more information.

© Women in Prison

KEY FACTS

⇨ Crime, its causes, and how it is dealt with, are some of the biggest issues in Britain today. Politicians and political parties can win or lose power depending on how well we think they are doing on the issue of crime. (page 1)

⇨ Two-thirds of the country believe that crime is rising when it is doing the opposite. (page 2)

⇨ According to British Crime Survey (BCS) Interviews survey in 2005/06, it is estimated that there were approximately 10.9 million crimes against adults living in private households in England and Wales. (page 3)

⇨ The risk of being a victim of crime as measured by the British Crime Survey (BCS), at 24 per cent, has increased by one percentage point compared with the year to September 2005 (23%). This is still considerably lower than the peak of 40 per cent recorded by the survey in 1995. (page 4)

⇨ 43% of those surveyed by Ipsos MORI think the murder of a child should be punished with the death penalty. 46% would recommend the death penalty in the case of murder in a terrorist attack. (page 5)

⇨ Britain is the most burgled country in Europe, has the highest level of assaults and above average rates of car theft, robbery and pickpocketing. Only Ireland has a worse record. (page 6)

⇨ There were 765 homicides in 2005/06, a decrease of 12 per cent from the previous year. This figure includes the 52 homicide victims of the 7 July London bombings. Homicide accounts for 0.06 per cent of recorded violent crime. (page 7)

⇨ Men aged 16-24 are most at risk of violence, at 12.6% of victims. (page 8)

⇨ 61% of crime victims surveyed by ICM did not feel that the use of prison reduced reoffending for the type of crime of which they were a victim. (page 10)

⇨ In one survey, eight per cent of all young people aged from 10 to 25 admitted to committing an offence six or more times in the last 12 months. They are therefore called 'frequent offenders'. (page 11)

⇨ Many young offenders are not only offenders, they are victims too. Being a victim makes many children more likely to commit crimes themselves. (page 13)

⇨ Boys are more likely than girls to report having negative contact with the police for the first time at age 12 or under. (page 14)

⇨ In the last 12 months, four per cent of all 10- to 25-year-olds had been arrested, two per cent had been to court accused of committing a criminal offence and one per cent had been given a community/custodial sentence or fine. (page 17)

⇨ 43% of those surveyed admitted to being 'very worried' or 'quite worried' about their own personal safety when they are out in their local area and see groups of teenagers hanging around the streets. (page 18)

⇨ Over 3,350 children and young people are being held in custody. (page 19)

⇨ Groups of teenagers 'hanging out' on the streets may look intimidating, but young people often gang together with friends as a way of keeping safe and avoiding trouble, according to a study of parents and children in disadvantaged communities. (page 20)

⇨ ASBOs can be used on any person over the age of 10 and can last up to two years. (page 21)

⇨ ASBOs were introduced in April 1999, aimed at tackling relentless low level street crime. However, 42% of ASBOs issued were breached in their first two and a half years. (page 22)

⇨ Overuse of ASBOs can lead to many youngsters regarding them as a 'badge of honour'. (page 23)

⇨ In a 2006 report, 90% of young people questioned denounced anti-social activities, and the majority accepted that swearing, arguing and loud music can be anti-social. 98% felt that the media always, often or sometimes represented them as anti-social. (page 24)

⇨ In 2005 more than 1.5 million Britons thought about moving away from their local area due to young people hanging around and 1.7 million avoided going out after dark as a direct result. (page 26)

⇨ 80% of people in a survey performed by the Audit Commission said they were not satisfied with the levels of police patrol in their area. (page 33)

⇨ A report published by the National Audit Office found that around 65 per cent in a sample of 893 people who received some form of anti-social behaviour intervention did not engage in further anti-social behaviour. (page 35)

⇨ In the ten years to 2003, the prison population increased by 66%; in the case of women, 191%. (page 37)

GLOSSARY

Age of criminal responsibility
In England, Wales and Northern Ireland, a child has to be 10 before they can be found guilty of committing a crime – this is the age of criminal responsibility. The age was lowered from 14 to 10 in 1998 and is lower than in many other countries. Children under the age of 10 lack capacity to commit a crime: the legal term for this rule is *doli incapax*.

In Scotland, the age of criminal responsibility is eight – one of the lowest in Europe.

ASBO
ASBO stands for Anti-Social Behaviour Order. It is a civil order against behaviour which causes 'alarm, harassment or distress'. It can cover things such as graffiti, shoplifting or frequently playing loud music. ASBOs are very controversial: although figures suggest they have a high level of public support, it has been claimed ASBOs are ineffectual and unfairly target young people.

Crime
Crime may be defined as an act or omission prohibited or punished by law. A 'criminal offence' includes any infringement of the criminal law, from murder to riding a bicycle without lights. What is classified as a crime is supposed to reflect the values of society and to reinforce those values. If an act is regarded as harmful to society or its citizens, it is often, but not always, classified as a criminal offence.

Criminal justice system
The system used by the Government to maintain social control, prevent crime, enforce laws, and administer justice.

Custody
In criminal terminology, being 'in custody' refers to someone being held in spite of their wishes, either by the police while awaiting trial (police custody), or, having received a custodial punishment, in a prison or other secure accommodation.

Detection rates
Detection rates, in their broadest terms, refer to crimes 'cleared up' by the police. Detection rates refer to crimes, rather than offenders. For example, if six offenders are involved in a robbery this counts as one crime. In 2005/06 there were around 1.5 million detected crimes in England and Wales.

Non-custodial sentence
A punishment which does not require someone convicted of a crime to be held in custody, in prison or another closed institution. Community service, restraining orders and fines are all types of non-custodial punishment.

'Paedophobia'
A term coined to describe the fear of young people which many think is becoming increasingly common. Young people in the UK often receive negative media coverage and can be associated unfairly with crime and anti-social behaviour by some adults.

Reoffending rate
The rate at which a person, having been convicted of a crime and punished, will then go on to commit another crime (implying that the punishment was ineffectual as a crime deterrent). 73% of young offenders aged 18 to 21 and 82% of young males aged 15 to 18 are reconvicted within two years of release from custody. These are known as repeat offenders.

Restorative justice
This usually involves a conference or meeting where the offender sits down with the victim, family members, and possibly other people from the community or people related to the crime. This means they do not have to make a court appearance. The purpose of the meeting is to discuss the offending behaviour and come up with ways for the person to 'repay' the victim or community for their crime.

'Smarter justice'
A term coined in a Home Office bill, referring to plans which the Government claim will rebalance the criminal justice system in favour of the victim.

Victim personal statement
This allows a crime victim to explain more about the impact of the crime on them personally. It can then be used by the judge or magistrate to help them decide on an appropriate sentence for the offender.

Violence
The World Health Organization defines violence as 'the intentional use of physical force or power, threatened or actual, against oneself, another person or against a group or community, that either results in or has a likelihood of resulting in injury, death, psychological harm, maldevelopment or deprivation.' There were approximately 2,349,000 violent incidents in England and Wales between 2005 and 2006. Weapons were used in 22% of all violent crimes reported in the British Crime Survey in 2005/06.

Young offenders
A young person who commits a crime between the age of criminal responsibility (10 in England and Wales) and their 18th birthday is classed as a juvenile offender. Between the ages of 18 and 20 (i.e. up to their 21st birthday), they are classed as young offenders.

INDEX

Additional Resources

Other Issues titles

If you are interested in researching further some of the issues raised in *Crime and Anti-Social Behaviour*, you may like to read the following titles in the **Issues** series:

⇨ Vol. 131 *Citizenship and National Identity* (ISBN 978 1 86168 377 9)

⇨ Vol. 130 *Homelessness* (ISBN 978 1 86168 376 2)

⇨ Vol. 128 *The Cannabis Issue* (ISBN 978 1 86168 374 8)

⇨ Vol. 120 *The Human Rights Issue* (ISBN 978 1 86168 353 3)

⇨ Vol. 114 *Drug Abuse* (ISBN 978 1 86168 347 2)

⇨ Vol. 108 *Domestic Violence* (ISBN 978 1 86168 328 1)

⇨ Vol. 93 *Binge Drinking* (ISBN 978 1 86168 301 4)

⇨ Vol. 92 *Terrorism* (ISBN 978 1 86168 300 7)

For more information about these titles, visit our website at www.independence.co.uk/publicationslist

Useful organisations

You may find the websites of the following organisations useful for further research:

⇨ Centre for Crime and Justice Studies: www.crimeinfo.org.uk

⇨ Economic and Social Research Council: www.esrc.ac.uk

⇨ Howard League for Penal Reform: www.howardleague.org

⇨ International Centre for Prison Studies: www.prisonstudies.org

⇨ National Youth Agency: www.youthinformation.com

⇨ Victims of Crime in Scotland: www.scottishvictimsofcrime.co.uk

⇨ Victim Support: www.victimsupport.org.uk

⇨ Women in Prison: www.womeninprison.org.uk

⇨ Youth Justice Board: www.yjb.gov.uk

ACKNOWLEDGEMENTS

The publisher is grateful for permission to reproduce the following material.

While every care has been taken to trace and acknowledge copyright, the publisher tenders its apology for any accidental infringement or where copyright has proved untraceable. The publisher would be pleased to come to a suitable arrangement in any such case with the rightful owner.

Chapter One: Crime

Crime and justice, © Centre for Crime and Justice Studies, Crime in the UK, © Economic and Social Research Council, Crime in England and Wales, © Crown copyright is reproduced with the permission of Her Majesty's Stationery Office, Britons most worried by crime, © Ipsos MORI, Britain tops European crime league, © Telegraph Group Ltd, Violence in the UK, © Economic and Social Research Council, Victims of crime reject notion of retribution, © Guardian Newspapers Ltd, Victims of crime survey, © ICM Research.

Chapter Two: Crime and Young People

Youth crime, © Centre for Crime and Justice Studies, Young offenders, policing and prisons in the UK, © Economic and Social Research Council, Young people and crime, © Crown copyright is reproduced with the permission of Her Majesty's Stationery Office, Attitudes towards teenagers and crime, © Ipsos MORI, Crisis in custody, © Youth Justice Board, Teen gangs, © Joseph Rowntree Foundation, ASBOs, © TheSite.org, ASBO mania, © Headliners, ASBO research published, © Youth Justice Board, The voice behind the hood, © TheSite.org, Positive press, © Headliners, Fear of young people, © Institute for Public Policy Research.

Chapter Three: Crime Solutions

Help! I'm a victim, © TheSite.org, How crime can affect you, © Victim Support, 'Smarter justice', © Guardian Newspapers Ltd, Reporting a crime, © Crown copyright is reproduced with the permission of Her Majesty's Stationery Office, Some reasons people don't report crime, © Victims of Crime in Scotland, The police, © Centre for Crime and Justice Studies, Police want new powers of 'instant justice', © Guardian Newspapers Ltd, Tackling anti-social behaviour, © National Audit Office, Going to court, © National Youth Agency, Why the prison system needs reform, © Howard League for Penal Reform, The basic rights of prisoners, © Liberty, World prison population – key points, © International Centre for Prison Studies, About women's imprisonment, © Women in Prison.

Illustrations

Pages 1, 10, 25, 36: Don Hatcher; pages 6, 24, 33, 39: Simon Kneebone; pages 9, 14, 26: Angelo Madrid; pages 22, 28: Bev Aisbett.

Photographs

Page 2: Carl Silver; page 13: Sara Hoffman; page 16: Joshua Coty; page 23: Jake MacDonald; page 27: Kat Callard; page 29: Davide Guglielmo; page 31: Mateusz Atroszko; page 34: Michal Zacharzewski; page 35: Elena Gjorgjievska; page 38: Helen Assaf.

And with thanks to the team: Mary Chapman, Sandra Dennis and Jan Haskell.

Lisa Firth
Cambridge
April, 2007